2001

Quick Ways

to Look and Feel Your Best

Carol Brockway

HARVEST HOUSE PUBLISHERS
EUGENE, OREGON 97402

2001 QUICK WAYS TO LOOK AND FEEL YOUR BEST

Copyright © 1993 by Harvest House Publishers
Eugene, Oregon 97402

Library of Congress Cataloging-in-Publication Data

Brockway, Carol.
    2001 Quick Ways to Look and Feel Your Best / Carol Brockway.
        p.   cm.
    ISBN 1-56507-003-8
    1. Conduct of life.   2. Spiritual life.   I. Title.
    BJ1581.2.B666   1993
646.7—dc20   92-19016
                                                            CIP

Printed in the United States of America.

Contents

The Ultimate Image

The Ultimate Image

Do you want to be more beautiful? What a question. I do not know anyone who would say, "No, I want to be uglier." And, of course, the first thing we think of when this question is asked is outward beauty—the way we look. To a certain degree, outward beauty is important because we tend to feel better about ourselves if we think we are presenting a positive outward appearance. However, the true beauty of a person comes from the inside. Since outer beauty is also important to most of us, I have presented many tips in this book to help you achieve that goal. The main goal, though, should be inner and outer loveliness working hand in hand for a better you.

Many of us feel we can never be beautiful physically because we perceive so many inadequacies in ourselves—the shape of our nose, our height, our hair, our size, or whatever. These negatives can cause us to give up, making outer beauty seem an unachievable goal. However, everyone has some beautiful features on which they can capitalize. The secret is having the knowledge and the confidence to camouflage figure flaws and imperfect facial features and then to highlight our best qualities. Remember, there are no perfect people and everyone has something they need to improve. With chapters from makeup to clothing tips this book will give you many ideas for achieving that outer beauty.

I remember an airplane flight I took from Idaho to California. The stewardess on this flight was a perfect illustration of how to use makeup, hair, and dressing techniques to bring out the best in oneself. When she approached me my first impression was how lovely she looked. However, when I took a closer look at her features, I realized that she should not have looked that attractive. Since I am in the beauty business, I began to look closer at the reasons she was so pleasantly put together.

Her nose was a little large and her eyes were a little too close together for the perfect face but her careful use of makeup techniques and a wonderful hairstyle took away from these problems. She had learned what to do to bring out her best features and downgrade the less attractive ones. She also looked very neat, clean, and tidy. She chose colors in her makeup and clothing that highlighted her skin tones. This woman also walked with an air of confidence because she looked her best. She was very kind and thoughtful and she had a smile that made you feel good not only about her but about yourself.

Most of us will never be Miss America but we can all be extremely attractive implementing some of these simple tips. This book will provide you with many ideas to help you improve your image both on the outside and the inside. Both outer and inner beauty go hand in hand for that positive image that touches and affects people's lives for the better. No one has perfect features, but life becomes fun when you set goals and begin to achieve them with changes that help you feel better about yourself.

A healthy diet and exercise program is important for both outer and inner beauty. When you feel well, it will shine out through you in a glowing complexion as well as a joyful spirit, so take care of yourself nutritionally. There are a multitude of good diet and nutrition tips in this book. Read them and begin to utilize them for a healthier you.

Set goals for outer and inner beauty and don't ever let anyone tell you that you can't reach those goals because with knowledge, determination, and perseverance you can become that person you have always dreamed of being.

God gave us an inner desire to look and feel good about ourselves and when we do we can give of ourselves to others in a more positive way. When I was working in the nursing profession, I learned that one of the first signs of mental distress and giving up was when the person began to no longer care about her appearance. And one of the first signs that she was getting better was that she began to care about herself by bathing more frequently and asking for makeup, a comb, and a mirror. Feeling good about ourselves is important to our overall well-being.

In the chapter on personality, much is said about the attributes of inner beauty and what makes a person pleasant to be around. When I was teaching, I loved the definition that we used to describe charm. I think it is a good definition of inner beauty. "Charm or inner beauty is the ability to make someone think that both of you are quite wonderful." A person with this ability is going to appear extremely attractive. The inner glow of someone happy with themselves shows outwardly in so many ways. A smile can warm a heart and certainly can add to a personality. In fact the experts on beauty say your beauty quotient goes up 50 percent when you smile rather than frown. Smile lines are upward lines and less aging whereas frown lines are downward and can age a face more quickly. Anger, harshness, and bitterness always appear in undesirable lines on the face as well as in your general attitude toward life. This is a perfect example of outer and inner beauty working positively or negatively.

There was a young woman in a beauty pageant I was judging who by all standards was one of the most beautiful girls in the contest. Outside beauty on this girl was premium but the way she treated others and the foul language coming from her mouth soon left that outer beauty lying at her feet. Of course, she did not even come close to winning the pageant. I am sure you have seen a physically beautiful woman who lacked inner kindness and a Christ like spirit and after you discovered this, her outward beauty faded. The opposite can be true of a not so physically attractive person who becomes truly beautiful and attractive because of the essence of beauty inside.

So many people today lack a proper self-image because of the emphasis put on outward beauty. This is certainly caused in a significant way by the media which says you must be young, five feet eight inches, have long lashes, a perfect nose, perfect hair, and of course, a perfect body.

This is why it is so important to see yourself in the Creator's eyes. He said that when He created you, the job was perfect because He is perfect and you were created in the image of God. So then, why do we question our worth and our looks? One of the reasons is because we see ourselves as our mother, father, teacher, or peers tell us we are rather than remembering God's creation and that each of us is a significant person. That doesn't mean that we don't need to change and be the best we can be on this earth, because that's what makes life exciting—to go up the ladder improving ourselves mentally, physically and spiritually. When we do changes begin to take place in our attitudes and actions. It would be very boring to get up in the morning and be so perfect that there would be no challenge to improve our image inside and out.

One of our most important beauty improvements should be how we treat one another and what kind of attitude we reflect to others. One of the places that our images could improve would be in our homes with our families. It is easy to let our hair down and take all of our frustrations out on the ones who we love the most but they should get the best of us not only on the outside but the inside also. However, home is usually where we look the sloppiest with the least makeup and where inside beauty is fleeting when we let small petty annoyances get in the way of enjoying our lives and our families.

It seems that when we are unhappy with ourselves, it is very hard to keep from taking our bad feelings and tensions out on those around us. Everyone has tensions and worries because there is no way to avoid them. However, it is not the problem but how you face it that counts. We have heard that said so often but nothing will change unless we truly let God sit on the throne of our lives and help us with all the frustrations of life instead of us trying to manipulate them ourselves. When we let God do the directing, our inner beauty improves and something seems to happen to our attitude. We can try and try to change ourselves on the inside but until we have a beautiful spirit allowing the Lord to be a part of our everyday living, true beauty from within can be elusive.

God tells us in Proverbs that outer beauty fades, but the beautiful spirit of a woman who fears the Lord will always shine (Proverbs 31:30). It would be my greatest joy if after my days on earth are finished, my family would say I was a blessing to them because of my godly spirit.

This book is filled with tips that are simple, easy to implement, and if followed will save you money. It is full of wonderful guidelines for both outer and inner beauty. Putting these suggestions into practice will lead to a more positive lifestyle.

Knowing these tips to achieve outward beauty brings a confidence we sometimes lack, and this helps to give us the inner beauty we seek by being the best we can be inside and outside. Our lives become balanced—inner beauty and outer beauty working together in a presentation pleasing to ourselves, other people, and the Lord.

——— ❧ ———

PART 1

Foundations
for Beauty

CHAPTER

1

Personality Plus

Charm is deceptive, and beauty is fleeting, but a
woman who fears the Lord is to be praised.
—Proverbs 31:30

Our image is reflected every day in our attitudes toward our work and toward other people. Many times people do not have a positive attitude because they are always fretting about what was or what might be. Since one cannot change the past and the future continues to march on, we might as well live as fully as possible in the here and now. We have a great power and that is the power of choice. We can choose to fret and stew or be inconsiderate and harsh. Or we can choose to relax and trust God to take care of our worries and give us a spirit of peace and joy even in the midst of trials. When we do this, our personality quotient will go up and the positive influence we have on our friends and the world around us will be evident.

Your inner attitudes are extremely important because attitudes can make you appear either beautiful or unattractive to other people, and certainly it affects your daily living. Your attitudes are a reflection of your inner feelings and are reflected in your smile, the way you greet someone, and the way you talk on the telephone.

One of the qualities most effective in influencing lives in a positive way is enthusiasm. It is contagious and makes a person appear to be in love with life, which in turn presents the new perspective that maybe life isn't so bad after all. Energy is beauty and is essential to being able to do the best in this world. It is not exciting to be around someone who is lacking the enthusiasm or energy to do things. Physical energy

11

not only comes from an enthusiastic spirit, proper food, and good health care but also springs from proper clothing and comfortable surroundings.

Negativism can really dampen the spirits of those around us as well as make us less likeable. A sour attitude about life and a critical spirit causes a person to lose beauty both inwardly and outwardly very quickly. Sometimes we recognize that our attitude is bad, but we feel too defeated to do anything about it other than nurse our hurts. However, this is when you should begin to put some of the following tips into play and talk to yourself about being pleasant even when you don't feel it. If you do, then soon you will feel better.

Inner Beauty

Inward beauty is one aspect that cannot be overlooked and one that radiates through our outward actions and speech. A lack of inward beauty can destroy our outward beauty. Inward beauty is a feeling of well-being. It's feeling fulfilled in whatever sphere of life you have chosen. This radiates to other people, making you extremely attractive.

Like snowflakes and roses, each of us was created unique and special. Each of us is different but beautiful in our own way. However, sometimes we let the everyday circumstances take the bloom off our rose, and when anger, harshness, and unkindness enter our lives, the inner beauty begins to fade. I had a friend who was like the Rose of Sharon. Her inner beauty bloomed with a smile and a positive word for me every time I was in her presence. One of the things that I remember the most about her was her wonderful laugh and attitude about life, even laughing at the adversities that had entered her life. She could always seem to find a little humor in a situation. I loved that and I loved being around her. She has gone to be with her Lord but I remember the last time I talked to her she was very content and happy.

Everyone gives off some kind of fragrance. God says in 2 Corinthians 2:14,15, "Thanks be to God, who always leads us in triumphal procession in Christ and through us spreads everywhere the fragrance of the knowledge of him. For we are to God the aroma of Christ among those who are being saved and those who are perishing." Fragrances float so we need to ask ourselves what kind of inner beauty fragrance we are spreading.

A beautiful inner spirit is reflected in our attitudes. There is so much negativism in the world today and inner beauty is fleeting when confronted with continual negativism. It seems that regardless of how good a job someone does, it is not good enough for some people and these kind of people can always find things to criticize. If you work in any kind of club or hold down any kind of outside job, it will not take long for this negative trait to become evident. Learn something from this attitude and do not have it yourself. Negativism can become a habit. Stop those negative thoughts and replace them with positive ones until the habit of negative thinking is broken.

I have a friend who is the epitome of a positive person and she has a beautiful inner beauty. She bore a son who had an incurable disease. This would cause a lot of us to ponder why and let it affect the way we look at God. Certainly our inner beauty could fade. My friend, however, never let a "poor me" spirit surround her or her family. Consequently, she has touched many lives by her example. Also, her son lived 20 years past his expected life span and I feel this was due in part to the positive spirit she taught her son to have in the face of adversity. Her secret was complete trust in her Lord. The Scripture from Philippians 4:6,7 tells us, "Do not be anxious for anything, but in everything, by prayer and petition, with thanksgiving, present your requests to God. And the peace of God which transcends all understanding, will guard your hearts and your minds in Christ Jesus." To try to change things in our own power brings frustration; however, letting God do the changing, whatever the outcome, brings peace knowing that it His way best. This is what she had learned. The difference between her and others I know is she really believed what God said was true. Many of us say that we do also, but we do not act like we do. Imagine what a happy and joyful life Christ is offering us if we will only trust and walk in faith.

All of us have frustrations and bad days and all of us feel pressures that make us less than sweet to be around. There will be less of those days, however, if the Spirit of the Lord is the guiding factor in your life. There are some people who are more pleasurable to be around because of their nature and personality whereas other people may find it harder, but all temperaments need the temperance of the Lord.

What do you do when you start to get upset with your surroundings and the inner beauty begins to fade? One of the best things to do, if at all possible, is to get away by yourself, if only for 10 to 15 minutes. Everyone needs time to themselves to reflect and cut out the noise and wear and tear of the world around them. Jesus preached and practiced this by going away by Himself to the opposite shore. Also, prayer and the reading of God's Word has proven to be one of the most calming factors in the face of adversity and problems.

Why not sit down today and have a good talk with the Lord and tell Him how you feel about yourself and what you would like to change and make different. God's wonderful gift to each one of us is Jesus Christ His Son. He can live in our hearts and guide our lives as well as temper our spirits if we give Him permission. It is as simple as asking Him to do so. Become God's woman by simply asking Him to come into your heart and life and take over the mess you have made, and ask His forgiveness for trying to do it yourself. If you sincerely do that, He will come into your life and help you become the person you desire to be. We are not taken out of trials, temptations, or frustrations but God will help us through them and give us triumph over them. Sometimes that is easy to say and hard to do. We are so used to carrying our own burdens and having our own way that surrendering completely in faith to God and letting Him have His way in our lives means that the control shifts from us to the Lord.

Sometimes it is hard to give Him my burden because I am afraid that God will not take care of it according to my plan and my timing. What I have found, however, is that when the crisis, problem, or worry has passed, God did know best. If God would have answered the way that I prayed, things would have really been a mess. Now I can look back and see how everything worked out God's way and it was so much better than my plans. God can take such bad situations and make them into a flower garden beyond our wildest imaginations. Romans 8:28 says, "All things work together for good to them that love God, to them who are the called according to his purpose" (KJV).

It is human to want to take the easiest route to solving problems that cloud our lives or to labor over what we should do to make things better. All of us have done this but the answer is to become God's woman or man and then to lead a life of obedience to Him and His Word. This is not a panacea to rid your life of problems, but when we obey God, He will bless and the inner beauty and peaceful heart we so desire will become reality.

We live in a complicated world and when there are so many things vying for our time and so many pressures crowding on all sides, it is hard to have the energy and time to pursue the type of lifestyle that brings less stress. A clear mind free of concern and full of God's love and guidance will make life much easier.

God has a plan for every life on this earth and seeking and living in that plan brings us the happiness and peace we all desire. Trying to live out of God's plan and trying to be beautiful from within on our own power, eventually brings frustration and the inner beauty we so desire becomes tarnished. Trying to improve our image inside without allowing the peace of God to reign will be fruitless and the unsettled spirit within us will keep us from becoming the person God intended us to be.

It is humbling to look at the world we live in and the complexity of creation and think that a God so omnipotent could care about you and me and our trials. But He does. The intricate petals of a flower are beyond comprehension but when you focus on these magnificent creations, it is certain that a God that powerful can take care of you and me.

———— 🐦 ————

Facial expressions are one of the most important body languages that we display.

•

A beautiful woman will avoid bickering, nagging, or criticizing.

•

A beautiful woman will use gentle feminine persuasion or compromise.

•

When you take time for yourself you will find that you are better able to give of yourself in a more positive way to the people around you.

•

Find joy in life by trusting God. Joy is the leavening in beauty but there are too many people who have pulled down the corners on their tight mouths. This is not only unattractive but also aging. There is not a more enchanting quality in this world than to be able to laugh at oneself. Being joyful is easy when you count your blessings and savor your joys whether big or small.

•

When you are really unhappy with yourself, be careful that you do not take your bad feelings out on others.

•

Inner beauty radiates kindness and love. An unloving and critical spirit is clear evidence that there is something wrong inside.

•

Take time for people and make their world a little happier for having talked to you that day.

•

The highest type of giving is done from the bottom of the heart.

•

When you speak, remember that God is listening also.

Emotions

God gave us emotions to spur us into growth. We all have highs and lows and, of course, we wish we could stay on the top of the mountain all the time. However, the lows in our emotional tide also bring growth and change. Both highs and lows work for our good. The emotions that should dominate the majority of our lives should not be the extreme emotions but rather the middle emotions. We need to use everyday challenges to develop emotional stability.

We feel much better about ourselves when the emotional part of our being is under control. Some examples of being under control are thinking before we speak in anger and turning the other cheek when responding to a negative comment; yielding a Christ-like spirit rather than uncontrolled anger.

Our attitude toward people and life in general is reflected in the way we walk, the way we speak, and certainly in our facial expression. You can make or break someone's day with a harsh criticism or a positive remark made with a smile.

One day the telephone rang and when I answered, a strange voice started into a magazine sales pitch. Since I was in a hurry and had no interest in the product, I was very short with the person. After I hung up, I felt bad about myself and how I had spoken to this salesman. This person was only doing his job and certainly did not deserve to have his day dampened by a rude customer. I have always remembered that feeling and learned something from it, and I have not been so rude again. What if it were your son or daughter on the other end of the line? The golden rule of doing unto others as you would have them do unto you is sound advice.

Energy Sappers

——— 🐾 ———

One of the top psychologists in the nation has patients that worry a lot keep a worry notebook. When they find themselves worrying about the past, present, or future, they are supposed to write their concerns in the notebook and appoint a specific time to fret about them later. Often the problems do not seem as big later.

•

Perhaps you have always wanted to do something that would require a bit of faith such as asking for a promotion or running for an office. Then fear steps in and says "What if I fail?" It is easier to sit back and feel negative and unattractive than to risk defeat. Force yourself to step out and do that thing that you fear. Some of the greatest lessons ever learned come from having to pick yourself up, step out, and do something that requires stretching beyond your comfort zone. It is far better to step out and improve yourself than continue in fear of failure and never try at all.

•

Worry saps energy so have a firm determination not to waste time and emotion on what cannot be changed.

•

Guilt feelings and self-pity are some other great energy time wasters. Realize that you serve a God who forgives you, cares for you, and gives you great worth.

•

Don't give in to anger because that takes a lot of energy and most of the time it is hard on your body as well. It takes longer to recover from anger than to get angry.

•

Don't harbor a grudge because it drains energy. Forgiving is healing to the soul. Harboring unforgiveness only hurts the one who doesn't forgive.

•

Your energy level as well as your mood is affected if you wear clothes that are uncomfortable. Do collars ride up on your neck? Are belts too snug and skirts or waistbands too tight? Are your shoes comfortable? All of these may be small points but they can sap energy.

Confidence Builders

——— 🐝 ———

Learn to do at least one thing exceptionally well.

•

Since there are enough people who will point out your short-comings, learn to focus on what you have done well and it will increase your confidence.

•

Your confidence will increase in direct proportion to the amount you have prepared yourself for a task.

•

Learn to give and receive compliments. Many people have a hard time receiving complements. The statistics show that people who have a proper self-image are able to accept compliments and praise much more gracefully than those who have grown up with feelings that they are not worth much. Remember, whether you are giving or receiving praise, a sincere compliment can be the first step toward friendship.

•

Keep a diary of all your achievements and list everything that you feel you have done well. When you do this, you will come to realize how much progress you are making toward reaching your goal.

•

Learn to be an effective touching person. The power of touching cannot be underestimated. By touching someone, we can affirm our friendship and approval, communicate a positive message, and promote good health. Unfortunately, many people avoid simple acts of touching such as a pat on the back, handshakes, and cordial hugs which all affirm goodwill. Everyone needs a hug a day.

Let your imagination flow.
Do creative things all year long
to make someone else happier and you
will end up being a happier person.

A critical spirit can tarnish your personality. It can become a habit, so be aware of your speech pattern and begin to correct any criticism.

•

People who lack meaning in their lives tend to be less happy with almost every aspect of their lives. This is why one person can be devastated by something that happens to them and another person with the same problem is able to rise above it.

•

Spend time with someone who makes you feel accepted and important to them. Everyone needs to continue to improve their lives, but that does not mean we don't need to accept people just the way they are. Feeling accepted is healing.

Stress Busters

The stress that is best for you is the one that will take you up to but not beyond your limits. Stress can be very productive, giving you the drive to create, strive, and achieve. It is too much stress that leads to tension and ill health. Balance is the key.

------ 🙠 ------

You have the ability to make or break someone's day by your attitude toward them as displayed by a simple smile or a cruel word. By the way, this includes your family. You would be amazed at how much stress can be reduced when there is harmony.

•

Read books and biographies of people who have succeeded.

•

Make some friendships and cultivate relationships with people who have positive qualities that add to your life instead of subtracting from it.

•

Don't rely on false stimuli or sedatives such as cigarettes, alcohol, sleeping pills, or tranquilizers. Take control of your life.

•

Learning to get your priorities in the right order is one of the first things that you need to do when you start to improve and take control of your life. Organize your priorities around the things that matter to you and recognize what you want to achieve.

•

Learn to be flexible and roll with the tides.

•

You need to take breaks during the day to recharge your batteries. Everyone needs a place where they can surround themselves with a pleasant environment.

•

Do not let the day go by without doing at least one thing that you really want to do, whether it is watching something special on television, taking a walk, or reading awhile.

•

Be discerning about what you put in your mind. For instance, watching too many shows on TV that discuss problems and all the negatives of life can create more stress and anxiety in your own life.

•

We have many blessings we tend to overlook. Take time to meditate on the good things in your life.

———————————— ❧ ————————————

Learn to ignore those things
that you cannot change.
When life gets to be too much,
take it inch by inch.

————————————————————————

Work on developing a good sense of humor. When you begin to look at the craziness of everyday situations, that sense of humor can make things look less dismal.

•

There seems to be a direct connection between physical activity and personal well-being. Exercise can make you feel better, relieve anxiety, help stress, and elevate your mood. There is a certain level of exercise that keeps people happy and this level varies with age and from person to person.

•

Develop a hobby which interests you.

•

Don't spread yourself too thin.

•

Create a special place in your home where you can renew your thoughts. It may be a comfortable rocking chair or the kitchen table, but take time to reflect and get things into perspective.

•

Simple pleasures and blessings that we often overlook could include a new idea we had for the day or simply relaxing with a friend.

Attitudes in the Workplace

Surveys show that those who are happy with their work are happy in general. Most people do not work extra hard just for the money. Instead they find it important to feel a sense of accomplishment in their work. Some people feel that if they are not in some prestigious occupation, they are not as important. However, it takes everyone working together in various jobs to make this world work. Be proud of yourself and do the best in whatever occupation you have chosen.

—— ❧ ——

If you do not have a regular job, it is important to find other ways to work such as in volunteer activities, hobbies, or whatever suits you best.

•

A homemaker should maintain strong feelings about the importance of her job because being a good wife and mother is the most important job a woman can have.

•

Aspiring people who are headed for the top should look like they are headed for the top. See chapters 17 and 28 for information on women's and men's wardrobes.

•

In the business world, do not leave people's needs dangling. Sometimes we think if we ignore a problem, it will go away, but it doesn't. This is good advice for bosses who are dealing with people in an office.

•

It is important in the professional world to join and support the association that represents your profession.

•

Do not get a reputation as a gossip or a troublemaker.

•

Realize that most people who have made it to the top had to start at the bottom.

•

Your attitude has everything to do with how pleasant your work will seem to you.

•

Don't take your work home with you all the time. Everyone one needs a break.

•

Use kindness, soft answers, and praise to turn an office into a pleasant workplace.

•

Make your little work corner personal for you with pictures and pleasant things you enjoy such as flowers.

•

Do not wish yourself in the other person's place because he or she has a better job, lives in a better house, makes more money, wears better clothes, drives a better car, or has better food than you.

Family

A wife who has compassion and kindness for her family and others and who truly gives of herself cannot help but be admired.

——— 🐝 ———

Before it is too late, become very aware of the kind of influence you are having on your children. Many times what you do speaks louder many times than what you say.

•

Be aware of positive or negative things being said to your children. Building a proper self-image in a child is so important and that self-image is affected by what is said to him or her.

•

One of the most important areas that a family should work on is having respect for each other and each other's property. Demonstrate respect and love in a husband/wife relationship by being kind, considerate, and sensitive to each other's feelings. Your children will learn from this example.

•

Be an example of a beautiful mother by demonstrating respect for yourself and by caring for your personal needs as well as your household so that your children will develop these same values.

•

Be aware that you are making memories every day. Are they good ones?

Happiness Is Giving

One important thing that makes us happy is doing things for others. Why not take time today to do something for someone else? There isn't anything that improves our image more than to be a loving and giving person.

———— ❧ ————

Cook an imaginative dinner for someone.

•

Bake goodies for someone and deliver them with a nice note telling that person what they have meant to you.

•

When you are cooking, fix extra dinner and freeze it so you will have it to give to a person who does not have much time or has been ill.

•

Write frequent notes to people expressing your love and appreciation.

•

Write a note sprinkled with your husband's favorite perfume and stick it in his lunch box, briefcase, or leave it on his pillow.

•

Perhaps you have a friend with a busy schedule or a lot of children who never has a chance for an evening alone with her husband. Volunteer to take the kids for a night so they can have a romantic meal in their home.

●

Do simple little things that give pleasure; like placing a flower in the bathroom, giving a gift, or doing something special for your loved one.

2

Put On Your Best Color

*[His father] gave him a special gift—
a brightly-colored coat.*
—Genesis 37:3 TLB

One of the best things that you can do for yourself is to find a good color analyst in your area and discover your color key. This will save you money and time over and over again because you cannot even start to coordinate a wardrobe or purchase makeup without knowing your proper color key. When you know what colors are best on you, it is much easier to put together a wardrobe that will extend and save you money. It takes the guesswork out of shopping because you will not have a barrage of various colors that do not go together.

There are a lot of people doing a lot of guesswork to try and determine their best color key. I have found, however, that the only true way is to be color draped with cloths so you can see what the colors are doing to your skin tone. Be sure that you choose someone who knows what they are doing.

Most people know instinctively which colors, cool or warm, look best on them, but their choices are influenced by hubby, mom, peers, and the fashion industry. What you have to determine is not if you like the color but if the color likes you.

It is fun to use the cool and warm colors together but in order to have a workable, coordinated wardrobe, the majority of accessories should be in colors that coordinate well and move through your wardrobe easily. It's very hard to put a rust skirt with a pink blouse, but it is easy to mix and match if you stay in the same color family.

Cool means that you will wear colors that have an absence of yellow or gold in their undertones. Warm means that the colors have a presence of yellow or gold tones in them. An example of this would be pink and peach. Pink is made by putting red and white together, but when you add yellow you will get varying shades of peach. Therefore pink is a cool color and peach is a warm color.

Consider the color you put in your hair so that it matches the undertones in your skin. If yellow does not look good with your skin tone then too many golden highlights in your hair will not look good either. Golden tones work best for the warm-skinned person and the ash blond tones work best for the cool-skinned person. Every one of you have either cool or warm colors in the undertones of your skin.

Cool Color Tips

A cool-skinned person will have pink, sallow yellow, blue, or olive in the undertones of their skin. Do not wear colors with yellow or gold undertones. Do wear colors with blue and white undertones. You can tell if a color has yellow in it by holding the color next to one that has a different undertone. For example, if you put different reds together, you can tell immediately which ones have yellow in them.

If you are in the cool category you will be further divided into summer or winter colors. Summer people who have softer coloring both in skin and hair will wear the softer pastels and winters, people with deeper hair color, will wear the deeper colors. An example would be soft pink versus hot pink or a soft mauve versus a deep burgundy.

If you have the more gentle contrasts, for instance a light-to-medium hair color and a medium skin tone (summer), then you will look best in the more gentle contrasting colors, but if you have strong contrasts in your hair and skin such as black hair and ivory skin (winter), then you can effectively wear much stronger contrasts in your colors.

Most black people are winters and look best with the absence of yellow and gold in their colors. They wear deep contrasting colors such as deep blue, red, or electric blue. Some are autumns, depending on the amount of yellow sallow tone or golden tone in their skin.

Warm Color Tips

A warm-skinned person will have peachy or golden tones. They will wear colors with the yellow and gold undertones such as orange and rust.

If you are in the warm category you will be divided into springs and autumns. The spring people will wear colors that have the clear yellow undertones in them and the autumn people will wear the muted yellow or gold undertones. An example would be a clear orange color for spring and a muted rust for autumn. Both can wear orange and rust—the difference is in the depth of the color.

More Warm and Cool Color Tips

The following are specific tips on colors for the various seasons. This does not mean these are the only colors you can wear. It is only a guide. When you look at colors for yourself, just remember that if you are cool in your skin tones, then you will look best with an absence of yellow in your colors. If you are warm in your skin tones you will choose colors with the yellow and gold undertones.

Cool Colors for Summer People

Pink is the key color.

—— 🙖 ——

Red—blue undertones such as blue violet, soft and deep rose, mauve, orchid, raspberry, plum, soft pink, red violet, soft rose red, watermelon, light soft pale shades of purple.

•

Green—gray green, blue grass green, soft mist green, jade, pastel blue aqua, medium blue green.

•

Blue—soft blues, gray and silver blues, powder blues, medium blue, periwinkle blue.

•

White or soft whites, rose beige.

•

Cocoa, rose brown, soft gray, navy, charcoal, taupe.

Cool Colors for Winter People

Red is a key color.

——— ❧ ———

Red—deep blue reds, burgundy, raspberry, fuchsia, deep violet, magenta, hot pink, true red, royal purple.

•

Green—deep forest green, winter green, emerald, hunter green, jade, deep black green, pine green, bright turquoise.

•

Blue—indigo, royal blue, electric blue, sky blue, iced blue, true blue.

•

Pure white

•

Black, charcoal gray, navy blue, medium gray, taupe.

Warm Colors for Spring People

Yellow is the key color.

——— ❧ ———

Red—clear orange red, peach, coral, salmon, apricot, clear violet, warm pastel pink, clear bright red.

•

Green—yellow green, warm mint, soft lime green, medium yellow green.

•

Blue—blue green, aqua, turquoise, clear robin egg blue, light true blue, light periwinkle.

•

Yellow—clear bright yellow, butter, daffodil, light clear gold.

•

Creme and off-white.

•

Ivory, light warm beige, camel, honey tan, medium golden brown, light clear navy.

Warm Colors for Autumn People

Gold is a key color.

—— ❧ ——

Red—deep orange red, orange, rust, deep coral, brick, deep peach, salmon, mahogany, pumpkin, tomato red.

•

Green—avocado, deep yellow green, olive green, jade green, lime green, chartreuse, moss green.

•

Blue—turquoise, deep aqua, periwinkle blue, teal blue.

•

Gold—yellow gold, mustard.

•

Oyster white, warm beige, camel, bronze, dark chocolate brown, coffee brown.

General Color Tips

Most of us have dressed ourselves all of our lives and never thought about the color we put on even though color can make us look healthy or ill, older or younger, tired or refreshed. When you wear your own best colors you will feel more comfortable and the colors will make your skin appear smoother, clearer, and glowing. The correct colors also minimize lines and circles.

—— ❧ ——

If you are wearing a color too deep or too light for your skin tone, balance it out with your makeup by adding softer shades or deeper ones.

•

Check out your wardrobe to determine what your color trend seems to be and then choose additions to go with these colors. If you know your color key, there will be no more guesswork.

•

The most mixable colors are those in the neutral families such as blacks, browns, navies, and grays. These may seem a little dull to you but they really are not when you add beautiful bright colors, prints, and paisleys to them.

•

Though it would not be best to wear dark blue and dark brown together, you could still put together two different color families in navy and beige using one dark and one lighter color.

•

Do not throw out any clothes because they are not the right color for you. Simply add accessories such as a scarf or blouse in your correct color so that it is close to your face and will be reflected off your skin. Gradually as you purchase new clothing you can discontinue using the incorrect colors. This process takes time. Consider it a five-year plan to eliminate the colors that are not best for you and gradually purchase into your own color key.

•

Do not take the color swatches that are best for you too literally. When you are matching fabric, it should be in the same color family but does not have to match exactly. It can be very frustrating when you have to match a color perfectly.

•

If you wear the incorrect color even though the garment is correct, it can make you feel out of balance and you may not feel comfortable in the outfit without even knowing why.

•

Some Common-Sense Color Tips

Many people do not think of color as an accessory, but it can be one of the most eye-catching accessories you wear

Sometimes people get compliments when they are not wearing their best color. This can happen when a woman has a knack for putting together an attractive look and the observer is actually complimenting her on what is being worn rather than on the effect of the color. Also, the observer may love a particular color or the outfit may be a very attractive style Generally speaking though, if you think back to those colors in which you have felt the best and in which you have received the most compliments, then you might have an idea which colors are best for you.

Color is not an exact science. It is not whether you look horrible or great in a color but rather which color is good, better, or best. However, some people do look less than attractive in certain colors because the wrong color tends to drain the color from their skin.

——— 🕭 ———

When choosing frames for your glasses, color should be a big consideration. Not only should the color blend with your wardrobe but it should also complement your skin tones. See chapter 18 on glasses.

•

There are many ways to wear color but a good rule to follow is to use one accessory of intense color in an outfit and that is generally enough.

•

Many bright colors used together in an outfit makes an entirely different fashion statement.

•

For a white shoe to look best, it should be worn with a predominantly white background or soft pastels. If you wear white shoes with something too dark it will be the first thing that other people see.

•

Your best colors do not change as you grow older except that the colors you wear can soften with age. However, you will never be a warm-skinned person if you were born with a cool skin tone.

•

If you get a tan, continue to stay in your color key, just wear some brighter colors. It's all a matter of balance.

•

When you hear the word *taupe* referring to a good basic color, the best way to describe it is gray-brown. When you look at it you can see both gray and brown.

•

Be careful of black because it is not necessarily slimming when it creates too definite a silhouette Medium to dark colors may be better. Make use of full-length mirrors to get an overall image.

•

Color is considered the number one factor in attracting a customer to a product.

•

Many women are very shy about color and stay in the same shades over and over again. When you know your color key, it helps you to step out with a variety of new colors to help perk up an otherwise dull wardrobe.

The colors that a person chooses to wear for the day can tell a lot about how they are feeling and thinking.

Some people think that they can't wear certain colors but you can wear a hue of every color if it has the correct undertone. The only exception is yellow. Some people do not look good in yellow at all. If there is too much sallow yellowness in the skin, wearing yellow will turn the skin more yellow.

•

As a general rule, brighter colors work best as accents except in play clothes and sportswear, and they are beautiful in blouses, sweaters, and scarves.

•

Achieve new looks in color by layering with two blouses in two different colors.

•

If you are a very small person, use three shades of the same color and keep it well blended. This is called monochromatic use of color and will add height to a short figure.

•

Pale shades give importance to a small figure.

•

Wearing variations in the same tone looks very sophisticated, especially in the neutrals like white, black, beige, or varying shades of blues.

•

If you have an olive complexion, avoid any of the beige colors that have yellow undertones.

•

The beige or taupe raincoat is the most professional color to lend status to your appearance. The beige would have the yellow undertones for the warm-skinned person and the taupe would have the gray undertones for the cool-skinned person.

———— ❧ ————

Learn to use color with skill and you can take moderately priced items or even some of your old clothes and blend the colors so expertly that the final outfit will look absolutely elegant. The neutrals—beige, tan, taupe, gray, black, white, and navy—are key for coordination, and the wide variety of shades in these colors are fashion classics and work well every year. They will never be unfashionable and they always appear elegant as well as being extremely versatile. They should constitute the framework of your wardrobe.

Color Perceptions

It has been said that color follows a pattern of the economic feeling in our society. When the times seem somewhat depressed, then the color scheme seems to follow with dull, depressing colors such as gray.

Studies show that colors seems to follow a cycle beginning with bright colors, then pastels, then basics such as black and white.

If Africa is big in the news the color trends for the season may follow the ethnic prints or yellow and green.

Scientists say that color is capable of affecting our moods, sensations, and even the way we will relate to the world. They have done tests to prove that color or the lack of it can affect our state of mind, reflexes, blood pressure, heartbeat, and respiration rate. Different colors can depress us, excite us, or even tranquilize us.

Because of this information, color is being used much more effectively in offices, restaurants, hospitals, and other businesses to achieve the proper effect on the client. The medical profession is also beginning to use color. Pediatric clinics cheer the small patient by adding bright, warm colors to walls and they use tranquil blues to help other patients relax more.

These studies say that it is important to take color seriously in our surroundings such as our home as well as our closet. Imagine if everything you looked at was gray.

Red

—— 🐛 ——

Red has the reputation of representing courage and it suggests an extroverted and optimistic personality.

•

Red is the color to wear when you want to draw attention to yourself because the eye will naturally seek out the brightest color in an audience.

•

Red is one of the colors that can be seen from far away.

•

Red is also the color to wear when you are shopping if you want to be waited on promptly.

•

Red comes on strong and a little goes a long way.

•

Some bright colors such as red are very expressive and give off a positive air. It can be used to show strength and persuasiveness.

Pink

—— 🐛 ——

When wearing pink, you are thought of as a little girl; nice but not too smart in business.

•

Though mauve, pink's cousin, continues the relaxed attributes of pink, it also adds stability.

•

If you dislike pink, you are a no-nonsense type of person who wants to know every detail.

•

It has been found that a room painted a certain shade of pink has a quieting effect on people who are agitated or violent.

Orange

——— ❧ ———

For many people orange is a great color when first seen but then becomes hard to accept. It has been said that orange personalities give great parties, are constantly on the move looking for something new, and change friends frequently.

•

Orange brings little negative association and is considered cheerful. Many extroverted people wear this color.

•

The muddier shades of orange, such as rust, are not as well liked and some people consider them cheap.

Brown

——— ❧ ———

Brown is earth's stable color and people who like brown tend to stay at home or at least in their own neighborhood. They are said to be frugal in their budgets and they get the most out of their money.

•

Brown does not test well in the business world, especially from the east to the midwest, and should not be worn in corporate business meetings in those areas. It seems to be accepted, however, in the West.

Green

———— 🖎 ————

Green is nature's color and is restful and nondemanding. The experts say that people who like green tend not to provoke arguments and to go along with the crowd.

•

Green is associated with tranquillity but only some greens are peaceful. Others, like olive green, cause negative reactions in people.

•

There has been some testing on green which says that it creates an air of suspicion about the honesty and integrity of a person. Therefore, it is said it is best to avoid wearing this color in professions dealing with finance.

Blue and Aqua

———— 🖎 ————

Aqua is said to reflect good taste and judgment. Many people like aqua and wear it well. Equal amounts of green and blue mix to make aqua and this color can be worn by everyone. If the color is a bluer aqua then it is best for the cool skin and if it is a greener aqua then it is best for the warm skin.

————————————— 🖎 —————————————

Navy or deep blue tells us that you are in command of a situation.

Blue is very restful and is said to have a calming effect on people. It is a good color for a bedroom.

•

Tests have shown that blue can lower blood pressure and ease anxiety.

•

Blue is associated with spiritual things and celestial things—probably because the sky is blue.

•

Some testing has shown that blue kitchens cause people to eat less than kitchens with bright warm shades such as yellow.

•

Blue is a cool color and is sometimes associated with sadness and trust.

•

Blue is one of the most favorite colors.

Yellow
—— ❧ ——

Yellow is said to be a color that can be seen farther away than any other color. That is why this is a good color for buses and road signs.

•

It is also said that yellow is identified with the mind and the intellect.

•

Yellow is a good mood-lifting color and therefore a good color to concentrate on for a few minutes if you are depressed.

•

Yellow is a color that is said to show confidence and composure as well as caring and giving.

Purple
—— ❧ ——

Purple makes people think of high rank and prosperity.

•

Purple is also one of those colors that people either love or hate There doesn't seem to be much feeling in between regarding this color.

Some General Perceptions About Color

The more subtle the colors and the color combinations that you choose, the less aware people will be of the influence those colors have on them. However, they are affected whether they are aware of it or not.

Our perception of color is often dependent on past associations and experiences. Research has found that the wrong colors in an office or factory can destroy employee morale and the right colors can increase productivity.

An interesting study was done on an airline. When the interior of the plane was upholstered in yellow green, there was a marked increase in airsickness.

Here is an interesting thought for you. Why do you suppose fast-food restaurants use the bright color combinations of yellow, orange, shocking pink, and red? Because it makes us move faster, salivate, and not linger over our food.

Be aware of how color affects many of our value judgments of people. On a first impression, a woman wearing a gray suit may be thought of as very conservative and businesslike, while a woman that is wearing a bright red dress may be thought of as exciting, stimulating, and very romantic.

•

Everyone reacts whether consciously or not to the colors you are wearing. If you wear a lot of white they think of you as pure and fresh.

•

When you wear all black you may be considered mysterious.

3

Diet and Nutrition

*Better a meal of vegetables where there is love than
a fattened calf with hatred.*
—Proverbs 15:17

It seems that everyone has been on some kind of a diet sometime in their lives. Everyone would like a magic wand to lose weight and inches but the truth is that it takes work, self-control, self-discipline, persistence, and consistency. When you think about it, if someone did have a magic wand it would not be as rewarding as having set a goal and then accomplishing it.

One of the reasons that people need to diet so much is because of their regular unhealthy eating habits. With so many fast-food places and so much junk food available, it makes it easy to eat poorly and easy to put on added pounds.

General Diet Tips

There are a lot of fad diets available that promote different ideas on losing weight, but the best way to diet is under supervision and with nourishing meals. Even low-calorie food is fattening in large quantities. There are some indications that frequent and overstringent dieting may affect the body's capacity to readjust to normal food intake once the diet is over. Realize that overeating is by far the greatest cause of obesity, and continual bouts of crash dieting are bad for the figure, bad for your health, and may turn out to be self-defeating. Weight loss on crash diets is usually attributed to losing water rather than losing fat. As soon as your body readjusts its water balance, you will be right back where you started. Crash or fad diets do not help those eating habits that need to be changed for you to experience a consistent weight loss. Slow and steady weight loss gives you time to discover your own weaknesses and strengths in relationship to food and gives your body time to adjust.

Don't fool yourself into thinking that once the weight is off you will simply stay that way. If you fall back into your old eating habits and ways of thinking you will probably end up back at your old weight. Diets have a high failure rate. Before you can break the vicious cycle of dieting and suc-cessfully manage to lose weight you must examine your attitudes toward yourself, the food that you eat or do not eat, and the various pressures exerted upon you by society. The most effective diet is a lifetime habit of intelligent low-calorie eating. This can become part of your lifestyle in far less time than you would think.

The amount of calories you need to maintain your body weight depends on several factors: activity, bone structure, metabolism, and climate. As we age we need fewer calories because our rate of metabolism declines and we usually are less active. There is some evidence that more calories are expended in colder climates.

One of the most effective ways for you to stay on a diet and lose weight is to set daily goals. Focus on losing weight one day at a time. Set up an exercise program and proceed one day at a time. If your end goal seems impossible, you can get discour-aged. The task will seem more achievable when you think of weight loss in small increments. Set inch-by-inch goals. Rewarding yourself for a five-pound loss is a more effective incentive than waiting until you have lost 20 pounds to reward yourself.

Don't just hope you can lose weight, but rather believe you can do it. To just hope you can do something is self-defeating. Get some determination and believe in yourself. Do not get discouraged if you slip once in awhile. While everyone fails occasionally, it is not a reason to give up and go back to your old ways of eating or to skipping your exercise regime.

There are many theories on how to diet and what to eat but until you determine in your own mind that you want to reach a goal weight you will not be successful. It doesn't matter what anyone says or how many helpful tips you get, you will not be successful unless *you* are ready to diet.

Identifying Eating Problems

——— ❧ ———

Make note of your eating habits. When you find yourself eating
at certain times other than mealtime, do some volunteer work
or plan some other activities to keep you away from the refrigerator. Many times we eat out of habit or because we are bored.
If you will keep busy, then you will not think of food so often.

•

Guilt can play havoc with how you see yourself when you feel
you are not doing enough. Do not let guilt rob you of what you
have accomplished. Every person has to start somewhere, so
don't feel guilty if you have to start slowly. For a woman who
has never exercised, working up to 15 minutes of exercise four
times a week can be a big hurdle. Just start doing something
because when you do nothing you feel guilty and that is defeat-
ing.

•

There are some occasions when dieting is impossible such as
at family get-togethers or on holidays and vacations. Learn to
cut back before and after the event and still enjoy yourself.

•

If you eat slowly and chew your food well, you will find that
you will eat less.

•

Skipping a meal is not a good idea unless you want to be twice
as hungry later.

•

Know your food weaknesses. We all have some, like chocolate,
cake, potato chips, etc. If you have a hard time giving up these
goodies, try freezing a candy bar and when the craving gets too
much, cut a small piece off and let it melt in your mouth to take
the edge off your craving.

•

Many of the experts believe that if you eat your food too rapidly,
your nervous system will not have time to warn you when you
are full. So try eating slowly, chewing longer, or taking smaller

bites. It takes 20 minutes for your stomach to tell your brain that you have had enough to eat. If you eat in less time, the message is not transmitted and you will still feel hungry.

•

It has been shown that people under stress eat more often, though not everyone responds to pressure by eating. To establish how stress-sensitive your appetite is, look back over your recent stresses. If you put on weight immediately afterward, then perhaps one of the keys to controlling your weight problem in the future is to simply be aware of how you react under stress and seek a different outlet.

•

When you are dieting, if you experience headaches before meals or when you have skipped a meal entirely, the cause could be low blood sugar brought on by an inadequate amount of protein and carbohydrate in your daily intake.

Healthful Snacks
—— 🐦 ——

Many calories are consumed in front of the television, so when you sit down to watch for an evening have on hand some carrot sticks, celery sticks, or some nonfattening food to munch instead of potato chips.

•

Keep your refrigerator stocked with good snacks such as fresh yogurt, fresh fruits, or fresh vegetables so that if the hunger pangs come you will have something to eat that is low in fat, easy to get to, and nourishing.

•

Suck a slice of lemon or dill pickle. The sourness will affect your tastebuds and may eliminate your craving for sweets.

•

Boost your energy level with a quick, nourishing snack such as cheese or an apple.

•

If you are counting calories, instead of having a calorie-laden soft drink, try iced mineral water with a slice of lime or lemon.

•

Add grapefruit to your diet because it stimulates faster digestion and fat-deposit breakdown.

•

If you are dieting and you crave a drink that is hot, try hot water and a teaspoon of unsweetened lemon juice instead of coffee. It has only three calories, tastes tangy, and works great as a natural diuretic.

•

Tomato juice has fewer calories than orange or apple juice. It has only about 25 calories per half cup, while orange juice has 55 and apple juice has 62.

•

Many people believe that liquids do not count in calorie totals in a diet. Tea and coffee are relatively free of calories but fruit juices, soft drinks, and alcohol are not and they can really add up quickly. Orange juice is good for quick energy and loaded with vitamin C but be aware that it is also loaded with calories.

•

Yogurt provides calcium in your diet, so eat a cup a day. Beginning in their teens and 20s, women need at least 1000 milligrams of calcium daily.

Achieving Maximum Benefits for You
——— ❧ ———

Always check with your doctor before beginning an exercise program and remember to use exercise and diets together for the maximum amount of benefit.

•

It is important to have someone who will reinforce your efforts and encourage you. It is hard to lose weight alone. This is why support groups like Weight Watchers are excellent. You may be a person that needs to be accountable to someone to be able to keep on your weight plan and reach your goal. If this is true, then lose weight on the buddy system. Find someone else who is on a diet or just a good friend, and share your feelings together. It is important to have people who will cheer you on and who will keep telling you that you can do it.

•

When you eat sugar, your craving for sugar is increased, so the best thing is to simply avoid it or at least keep it to a minimum. Sugar is not good for your digestive system anyway.

•

There are substitutes for sugar such as raw honey. When substituting raw honey in your recipe, use half a teaspoon of baking soda per cup of honey and one or two tablespoons less liquid.

*Avoid long-term diets,
especially those ones that advocate
a bizarre or highly restricted
range of food.*

You can look pounds thinner if you learn to dress with the correct line, style, and color. See the chapter on figure problems.

•

Do not start your diet on the weekend. It is best to start on Monday and then by the weekend you will be better able to adapt to it and will not be so tempted to go off the diet.

•

Be sure that you eat balanced nutritional foods from the four food groups.

•

Start your meal with soup and salad and it will cut down on the regular food that you eat.

•

It is unwise to skip meals, not only because of the nutritional loss but also because your metabolism slows down and consequently you do not burn up the fat. When you eat three planned meals a day, you keep the fat-burning process going. Or you can try eating six mini-meals instead of three regular ones. Nutritional balance is more important when you are slimming and eating considerably less than you normally would.

•

Do not recklessly start on miracle diets with no consideration for their nutritional value. You may end up poorly nourished and in a less-than-optimal state of health. Beware of diets that are dangerous because they limit the number of nutrients, eventually causing the body to take the nutrients it needs from its own cells.

•

Be a bit skeptical when reading the latest diet fad or wonder food. Unless they are prescribed by your doctor, avoid slimming aids that may affect the normal function and metabolism of your body.

•

It is important to drink plenty of water, preferably eight to ten glasses a day, and avoid diets that suggest you should restrict your fluid intake. The body loses about three to three and one-half pints of water a day and it is essential that this fluid is replaced. The less you eat the more fluids you should drink.

•

Sucking on an ice cube satisfies the urge to snack without adding calories.

•

If you want to lose one pound a week you have to cut your present calorie intake by 500 calories a day.

•

Diets that focus on one particular food will leave the dieter without energy and will give the dieter dull, brittle hair.

•

Unless you have all the willpower in the world, it is harder to stick to a diet that is complicated.

•

If you find you cannot eat just a little, then avoid having your danger foods around at all.

•

If you gain a few pounds back, do not let your weight stray too far before losing again.

•

Do not eat hot dogs on your diet. Sometimes they cause headaches because of the food additives such as sodium nitrate and nitrite processors.

•

When you are cooking dinner, chew sugarless gum or hold a toothpick in your mouth to remind you not to taste the food.

•

Exchange low-calorie recipes with friends or walk with someone in the mornings or evenings who has the same goal.

•

It is very important to cut down on fats in your diet not only for weight control but for your heart health also. Fat has over twice the calories of protein or carbohydrates.

•

Turn down second helpings and rich desserts

•

Yo-yo dieting where your weight goes up and down is worse than maintaining a consistent weight, even if your weight is a little higher than recommended.

•

Try to make a rule not to eat after 6 P.M. Generally speaking your body does not have time to burn up the extra calories before you go to sleep.

•

Try substituting quality for quantity in food. If you are eating less, perhaps you can afford the less fatty cut of meat.

•

Since fish is one of the best mainstay foods for a person trying to lose or maintain weight, get a recipe book with some good fish dishes in it and add this food to your menu

•

One key to successful dieting is your ability to shake the salt habit. Salt causes you to retain fluid.

Breakfast Diet

When you eat sugar for breakfast, it sends your blood sugar rate on a roller coaster ride and when your blood sugar falls, then your energy level falls also. This can leave you feeling irritable, depressed, and tired. If you continue unhealthy habits even though you may feel okay now, it will eventually catch up with you.

The traditional breakfast of bacon, egg, and toast is not a necessity. A good breakfast should consist of fruits, vegetables, carbohydrates, and protein. Try stepping out of the tradition by eating a piece of toast with peanut butter or a tuna fish sandwich.

Leftovers, such as a slice of quiche or cold fruit salad, make a great breakfast treat.

Get out of the old breakfast routine and serve soup or a nutritional breakfast salad Take the boredom out of breakfast

•

Try a breakfast shake which takes only a few minutes to prepare in your blender. Combine 1 cup of milk, 1 egg, 1 cup of strawberries or 1 medium banana, and 1 tsp. of vanilla

•

Try a cottage cheese sundae and top it with your favorite fruit and sunflower seeds Canned fruit is very good on cottage cheese when fresh fruits are not in season Buy the canned fruits with reduced sugar.

•

Keep some wheat germ flakes on hand to sprinkle on your toast or cereal to add some extra vitamin B to your diet. Wheat germ flakes need to be kept refrigerated.

•

The morning meal is about the most important of the day. Your body has been without food for many hours and it needs to be refueled. However, coffee and a jelly doughnut are not what your body needs.

Shopping Ideas
—— 🐟 ——

Get into the habit of reading labels on the foods that you buy and be aware that the ingredient listed first is the one with the highest content. If sugar is listed first on a cereal box, it contains more sugar than the other ingredients. Some cereals are 50 percent sugar.

•

Plan ahead so you can shop for foods thoughtfully with a list from which you do not deviate.

•

Never go grocery shopping with an empty stomach.

•

When purchasing food from the supermarket, instead of buying those products that are labeled "light," look for products that are marked "low calorie" or "reduced calorie." Reduced-calorie products must have at least one-third fewer calories than other similar foods.

•

Look for labels marked "low fat."

•

Read all of the label because sometimes the protein and vitamin content is reduced along with the calories.

•

If there is a brand-name food you use regularly that does not list the nutritional information, buy a different brand that does

Tips for Better Eating Habits

It is important for you to find a brand-new food plan that will fit in with your lifestyle and it is essential for you to know the calories that you need to maintain your ideal weight and feel well. Get some expert advice on where to start and how many calories your particular body needs to lose weight and maintain a healthy lifestyle.

———— 🐾 ————

Try keeping track of the calories you have resisted during the day rather than the calories you have eaten.

•

Do not eat anything unless you are sitting at the dining room table. This includes everything from dinner to a cracker.

•

Since it is always good to have your goals and your progress on paper where you can see it, make yourself a weight chart on graph paper and keep it where you can check your progress.

•

Give yourself rewards for reaching weekly goals. Keep a nicely wrapped nonfood reward for yourself in the refrigerator so that every time you open the refrigerator you will see it waiting for you. When you reach that short-term goal you take your reward. Then set another short-term goal, put another reward in the refrigerator and go for it. One lady said she did this and it worked so well that she went one step further. She gave herself a time limit and if she did not reach her short-term goal by the time allotted, she had to give the reward away.

•

Try fooling your stomach by eating more slowly. It will seem like you have more food. Also, try spreading your calories over five small meals rather than three large ones.

•

When the portions are small, serve them on smaller plates and give larger portions of low-calorie foods like salads.

•

Keep a diet diary to log your eating habits. Be very honest and use this diary to determine the best steps to take in keeping on a weight loss program. You may be eating more calories than you realize. Calories even from just a bowl of cereal can add up much faster than you realize.

•

Many times we eat just because it is time to eat. This may call for a lifestyle change such as doing something on your break from work other than eating. If it is hard to say no to the doughnuts at that time, try taking a walk in the fresh air.

If you have been losing weight,
then treat yourself to a new outfit.
The compliments that you get
will inspire you to continue.

If you will store all of your favorite cakes, cookies, and other goodies in opaque containers in an inaccessible place, it will help curb your sweet tooth. Another deterrent to eating these kinds of treats is to make the package difficult to open. Staple the potato chips bags and cookie bags closed.

•

Since carrot and celery sticks can get boring even to the most dedicated vegetable eaters, try a small box of raisins or a cup of plain popcorn.

•

Our bodies are 70 percent water so we should be eating a diet that is high in water content. This includes fruit and vegetables which should be predominant in the diet. The other 30 percent can be foods that are more concentrated such as breads, meat, dairy products, and grains.

Staying on Your Diet at a Party

When you are at a friend's home, do not think that someone will be offended if you do not eat all of the foods that are served. Chances are that they probably do not even notice.

———— 🐛 ————

If a host or hostess is continually offering you food, it is not offensive to simply say no thank you. A good host or hostess would not force someone to eat something they did not want or invite a diabetic to eat chocolate.

•

Try to position yourself as far away from the food as possible. The closer you are to the snacks the easier it will be to have just a little.

•

Carry around the same soda all evening and no one will even know if it is your first or second.

•

If it is a dinner party, use techniques such as eating very slowly. This way you will not have to refuse seconds.

•

De-emphasize the food and concentrate on other things such as seeing friends, enjoying conversations, and meeting new people.

General Nutrition

The body is an organism that continually renews itself. It needs good nutrition to rebuild cells and beauty requires a well-balanced diet. If you begin to look drawn and tired in the middle of a diet, do not worry. That drawn look will be gone in a month or so after your body fat redistributes.

The continuous eating of the wrong things may eventually result in some kind of disease. It is much easier to prevent something than to try to cure it.

Many diets end up being deficient in calcium. Calcium is a very important part of our diet and keeps our bones and teeth healthy. It starts leeching out of our bones in our mid-twenties and this causes one of the major aging ailments called osteoporosis. To prevent this you must build up a healthy calcium reserve. One study showed that the calcium intake of women averaged 12 percent below the recommended daily dietary allowance. Women are eight times more likely than men to develop osteoporosis. One of the reasons is that pregnancy and breast-feeding divert calcium from mother to child and another reason is that women are more likely to go on weight-reducing diets, many of which are low in calcium. Also, women have less bone mass than men.

———— 🕮 ————

Keep your vitamin B level up with beef, fish, broccoli, brussels sprouts, chicken, and cottage cheese.

•

A calcium deficiency can cause low moods so be sure your diet includes sufficient amounts of cheeses, milk products, beans, and broccoli.

•

Do not drink cup after cup of black coffee just because it has no calories. Coffee can destroy thiamine or vitamin B1 and cause a blue mood to get worse.

•

Some major sources of calcium are milk, milk products, cheese, ice cream, and low-fat yogurt as well as many vegetables.

•

Eating more protein than your body needs accelerates calcium loss.

•

Make sure that you get enough vitamin D through sunlight or diet because it aids the body's absorption of calcium.

•

If you do not have enough carbohydrates in your diet, you will become tired because your body is forced to burn up too many necessary fats. Prevent this by eating carbohydrates, proteins, and vitamin B.

C H A P T E R

4

Exercise for Good Health

Run in such a way as to get the prize.
—1 Corinthians 9:24

One medical professional said that you can run on adrenaline until you are 40 but after that you pay a high price for no exercise. If you will be faithful to an exercise regimen, whether it is jogging or walking home from work, it will pay you over and over again in the extra energy reserve it builds for you. Think big but start small. One new exercise may be all you can handle at the moment. Be sure you pick an exercise you like to do or you will never do it.

Exercise can burn those extra calories from eating things that you should not have eaten. Exercise burns up fat, makes muscles lean, and helps you maintain your weight a lot longer.

Headaches can be caused by an exercise program that is too strenuous. The smaller blood vessels do not expand fast enough to accommodate the stepped-up blood flow and headache pain can result. The solution is to slow down.

Often there is not enough time to do everything you need to do and adding an exercise regimen can seem unrealistic. Try using your lunchtime and break times for a brisk walk or even a little jogging in place.

•

Try sneaking some exercise into your day by standing instead of sitting, walking quickly instead of shuffling along, and using the stairs instead of the elevator or escalator.

•

The common complaint of women is that the accumulations of excess fat always seem to go to the thighs. Three of the best exercises for the thighs are swimming, playing tennis, and racquetball. You use the whole leg in these sports.

•

If you do not seem to have time for exercise, use all your time to advantage and stretch whenever and as often as you can. Stretching is a good exercise. Stand as tall as possible; lift your arms up and try to touch the ceiling with your feet remaining flat on the floor. Do this stretch at least four or five times a day and work on good posture.

•

Bicycling is a good muscle exercise and a stimulant to the circulatory system. This is a good activity to do as a family.

•

The people who need the exercise routine the most are the ones who come home too exhausted to develop a routine.

Walking

Walking is the closest thing to a perfect exercise and it can be done by almost anybody, young and old. All it requires is a good pair of walking shoes. It is nature's way to help with excessive tension, nervous strain, anger, or frustration. Try walking home from work if it is not too far and if it is safe. Walking helps you work off the daily tensions because you do not have to concentrate and because it is natural and automatic. It is an aerobic exercise causing you to breathe deeply while your heart beats faster. Walking can lower blood pressure caused by stress and is a natural tranquilizer which reduces anxiety and tension. Walking improves the muscle tone in your legs. A noted cardiologist said that he felt this form of exercise was one of the best because it provided more blood to the brain and helped people relax and think more clearly.

———— ❧ ————

When you exercise be sure that you choose the correct shoes What you wear is very important, so choose something comfortable that lets you move with ease. Good walking shoes should support and cup your heel, support your arch, protect the ball of your foot, provide traction, and allow your sole to flex for each pushoff.

•

Walk at a specific time every day so that it gets to be a habit.

――――――――――――――― ঽ৶ ―――――――――――――――

Get your spouse to walk with you
for it is a good time
to spend together in this
busy world.

If you stroll along slowly, stopping to talk to people or smell the flowers, you may feel relaxed at the end but you will not accomplish much in terms of fitness. For aerobic exercise, swing your arms, hold your head up high, and walk fast enough to make you breathe deeply.

•

Even if you do not work out of the home, instead of sitting down for a chat with your neighbors, ask them to go for a short walk with you around the block.

•

Start thinking of places where you can walk instead of ride like walking up the stairs instead riding the elevator.

•

When it is hot and humid, dress accordingly. Wear cotton because cotton absorbs perspiration and lets the excess moisture evaporate as you walk

•

In cold weather the opposite is true Dress with layers of clothing that trap the warm air and hold it next to your body. The more you walk, the warmer you become

•

A study at one university showed that a 15-minute walk reduced tension more effectively than tranquilizers.

•

Join the walkers at the malls. Often these mall-walkers have an organization you can join featuring special speakers. You could make some new friends this way.

Other Exercise Suggestions

—— 🐌 ——

One good indoor exercise to keep us from getting too flabby is jumping rope. It is a good aerobic exercise that can actually burn more calories than jogging. It requires very little space and no special expensive equipment except a rope and a good pair of shoes. When you jump rope be sure that you jump on a surface that does not cause too much jarring to the spine. To prevent injury it is always good to read up on the exercise you are planning to do.

•

If you have stairs at your disposal, run up and down the stairs. This is tougher than running on level ground so you get a better workout.

•

If you like music, turn on the radio or stereo and dance till your heart's content. Let yourself go and really move your arms and legs. This can really work up a sweat if you give it all you have. This is fun to do while you do housework.

•

If you have the space and money, purchase an exercise machine like a stationary bicycle or rowing machine. These can be very beneficial especially in inclement weather. When you work out on these, you can read a book or watch television and the time passes quickly.

•

Another good exercise tool is the rebounder. The secret is to not let the equipment collect dust but to create a consistent work-out routine that works for you.

•

There are some good exercise videotapes available, but be careful to purchase only those that are in your ability range.

Winter Exercise
—— ɞ ——

To get the most body benefits out of a winter walk, walk briskly. Most experts recommend that you walk at about four miles per hour. Check your pace by timing how long it takes you to walk one mile. Twenty city blocks equal one mile. At that speed you will burn about 300 calories an hour, you will begin to see your derriere and legs tighten, and you will improve the efficiency of your heart. In the wintertime, warm up by walking slowly for three to five minutes and then increase your pace by taking longer strides while swinging your arms. If you find the winter weather too cold for you, check the local mall or school for walking facilities.

•

Skiing is a fun exercise and it strengthens the thigh, derriere, and stomach muscles. It is very important to get in shape before you hit the slopes.

•

Cross-county skiing is good for the whole body and is rated one of the best aerobic sports. You will burn up about 600 calories an hour. Getting out in the country among God's creation can do wonders for stress levels also.

•

If you do not want to spend money buying ski equipment, you can rent. A cheaper winter workout may be just simply putting on a good pair of snowshoes and taking an invigorating hike through the snow-covered wilderness.

•

Snowshoeing is not as good aerobically as cross-county skiing but it helps develop leg muscles, increases your endurance, and will burn up about 400 calories an hour.

•

Use water in your exercise program. When it is too cold or too hot to walk or jog, use a pool and jog in the water.

•

To tone the arms and chest, rest the arms just beneath the water surface and push down and back as far as you can.

•

Always warm up before exercising to prevent the risk of injury.

Vacation and Exercise

When you are on vacation it is harder to keep up your exercise routine so incorporate exercise into whatever you are doing. If you are at the beach, go swimming. Rent a boat and go rowing. Or jog in the sand on the beach. If you are in the mountains, go for some hikes.

———— ————

Look for places that have a pool.

•

Play tennis and golf.

Bring some of your aerobic exercise tapes or check the television schedule for an exercise show.

Of course you can always go walking but you need to know the area and you should not go alone. Incorporate your walking into sightseeing. Do not ride everywhere you want to go.

•

Exercise in your room.

•

If you will exercise after a long trip it will help you get over the effects of jet lag and the fatigue of sitting in a car or on a plane for hours. Different things affect you when you travel such as time zones, climates, temperatures, plus various altitudes. Be sure to allow your body to adjust and do not push it too hard.

•

Do your stretching exercises before sleep. Make a note of how your cat stretches to see how you should do stretching exercises. The movements are slow and easy. Extend your muscles as far as you can without jerking and then reach a little further. Then, before you get out of bed in the morning, stretch like a cat. Remove the pillow if you use one, and inhale deeply on your back. Stretch each side of your body a few times as you breathe deeply so that you can get more oxygen into your blood.

General Facial Exercises

One area that people fail to exercise is the face and neck and this is where aging shows up first. Tiny muscles shape the expression of your face. They provide the underlying support structure for the skin and help keep it firm and youthful. However, no muscle remains firm without use so exercise your face muscles to keep them firm. Do not stretch the skin.

——— ❧ ———

If you are anxious or tense, it will show on your face when you set your jaw. You will find it hard to remain in this tenseness if you can laugh so try making faces at yourself. Laughter is a wonderful exercise for the face and body and one of the best ways of getting tummy muscles into shape.

•

Crunch your face up into your nose as though you have smelled something unpleasant.

•

Open your mouth and eyes as wide as you can and stick your tongue out to help your throat muscles. Release and do a silent scream.

•

Move your lips to the left and right and follow with the biggest grin you can muster.

•

Open your eyes up wide and see if you can make the grin stretch from ear to ear.

Neck Exercises

—— ?? ——

Tuck in your chin and pull in your lower lip and this will help firm the muscles at the front of your neck.

•

Hold your head correctly; not too far forward nor too far back because this can create tension in those muscles that connect the neck to the shoulders.

•

Posture is one of the most important factors in keeping the neck free from tension and stiffness, so check to see that you are sitting with correct posture.

•

Exercise the neck with exaggerated chewing motions. You can feel this by using the muscles around the mouth and neck.

•

The secret of success for any exercise program is to keep at it because the most effective exercises will do little to tone muscles if they are stopped after a few days or weeks.

Double Chin

—— ?? ——

Watch your posture and hold your head up.

•

Do not read in bed with your chin down toward your collarbone.

•

It is best to sleep without a pillow or to use a very flat one.

•

Stick your tongue out and try to touch it to your nose.

5

Put Your Best Foot Forward With Good Posture

I broke the bars of your yoke and enabled you to walk with heads held high.
—Leviticus 26:13

One area that can really add to your appearance and beauty is your posture. Good posture means having a beautiful carriage and the benefits are an appearance of confidence and good grooming. It also is an aid to healthy body-functioning, improves speech because the lungs and diaphragm have room to function properly, and gives a youthful appearance. When someone enters a room slouched over with their head down it automatically gives the appearance of old age, so keep your head up and walk with a gait that shows health and happiness and you will look and feel younger. We talk so much about clothes, hairstyle, and makeup and neglect a very important beauty aid—our posture. Good posture presents an illusion of beauty that can show a positive or negative message.

Some Reasons for Bad Posture:

Lack of posture instruction in the formative years.

•

Bad habits. You have had bad posture for years and need to work on changing your bad habits to good habits.

•

Soft chairs and mattresses can cause bad posture.

•

Not taking the time to walk and stand correctly will result in poor muscle tone.

Ways to Correct Your Posture:

—— ❧ ——

Practice correct techniques for reaching and stooping that keep your back straight. Reach forward or stoop downward to pick up something by bending your body at the hip and the knee sockets while keeping your back straight.

•

Be taller and slimmer by standing against a wall in good posture and trying to walk that way. See if you can keep the feeling of a straight back.

•

Hold in your abdominal muscles.

•

Your legs should swing easily from your hip joints when you walk. There should not be a wide stance with a lot of space between your legs.

General Tips

Most people from their childhood have learned to stand, sit, and even rest incorrectly.

To follow these tips you will need an awareness of how you are actually carrying yourself and you will need to take some action to change some very bad habits to goods ones. When you are aware of the things you do incorrectly, then you can begin to change them. Many times a lovely woman destroys her whole look of beauty by sitting incorrectly. Poise is lost if she sits with her lower limbs wrapped around the chair or even if she twists her legs into an awkward position.

—— ❧ ——

Poor nutrition and poor posture go hand in hand. Poor nutrition weakens the muscles and connective tissue so that poor posture results, and poor posture deprives the muscles of the circulation that would bring them the nutrition they need.

•

Posture delivers a message that says much about how people feel about themselves. Your outlook on life is tied to the way that you carry yourself. When you are weighted down with worries, then your posture tends to look the way you feel.

•

Keep the three heavy sections of your body squarely over each other. The right carriage not only makes your body its most beautiful but also its most efficient. Proper balance and movement decrease body fatigue about 80 percent.

•

Proper posture can whittle away pounds in appearance and give you the firm upward lines that are more youthful rather than the sagging lines of old age.

•

If you will lift your body upward, straighten your shoulders, and hold your head up when you are depressed or discouraged, it will help your spirits to lift also.

•

When you are standing, it is important to keep your weight equally distributed. Stand with your feet pointing straight ahead and not too far apart with the weight distributed evenly between them. When you put more weight on one foot, you tend to swing your body left or right and it immediately takes you out of proper body alignment.

•

Your arms with your elbows slightly bent should fall loosely and comfortably at your sides. Your hands should be in profile. If the backs of your hands are forward, it will round your shoulders and add width to your body.

•

Pull in your abdomen, straighten your lower back, and tuck in your derriere

•

Keep your head up, pull up your rib cage, relax and drop your shoulders.

•

Walk toward a mirror so you can detect some of your bad habits.

•

If you are aware of what you look like when sitting with your knees apart, you will not let this posture infringement happen again.

———————————— ❧ ————————————

It is possible to look one-half inch thinner in the waist by standing correctly.

———————————————————————————

Try closing your eyes and imagining that you are being pulled by a string from the top of your head. This should make your whole body lengthen and straighten.

•

Ballet is an excellent tool to help poor posture. Any kind of dance training that strengthens your supporting muscles will be beneficial to your posture. Most dancers have enviable posture.

•

Other beneficial activities that build strong bodies and encourage better body alignment are swimming and aerobics.

•

Good posture gives you a better self-image. Begin observing posture in people and see how they come across when they have correct alignment or what kind of image is portrayed when their heads are down and their shoulders are stooped.

•

How are you sitting now while reading this book? Are your shoulders in line with each other and your back straight, or are you slumping forward with your neck curved and your spine rounded, and one shoulder higher than the other?

•

Holding your head correctly influences the position of the vertebrae not only in your neck but also all the way down your spine. If you hold your neck in a set and rigid manner, it can lead to shortened and strained neck muscles which can lead to tension headaches and even migraines. You can release tension by holding your head correctly.

•

Aches and pains in the upper back can be caused by holding your shoulders incorrectly. Bring your shoulders level by standing with your weight evenly balanced on both feet and holding your head in a central position and bringing your arms to your sides. This will pull you into proper body alignment.

•

Be aware of the way you hold yourself when you walk in heels. The way you walk shows poise and beauty. High-heeled shoes pitch the body forward on to your toes and cause your hips to rotate inward to compensate for the unnatural angle of the feet, so it is best to wear a moderate or low-heeled shoe for everyday use.

•

When you are standing, walking, or running, your ankles should be slightly flexed to take the weight of your body and to act as shock absorbers.

_____

Here are some questions to ask yourself to help you become aware of your own personal posture:

——— 🕭 ———

Does your chin jut out or do you tuck it down and back or tilt it upward?

•

Do you see a dowager's hump beginning at the base of your neck from jutting your head forward?

•

Are your shoulders tense and sometimes hunched forward making your neck tense?

•

Is the part of your back just below your neck straight or slightly curved?

•

Do you have a pot belly no matter how thin you seem to get?

•

Do your arms hang in the front of your body rounding your shoulders?

If you answered yes to any of these questions you need to check your posture. If your shoulders and head are not held in a straight line, your back won't be straight either and your abdomen will start to pooch out. If we use incorrect posture for a long period of time, some parts of our body can acquire deformities such as the dowager's hump. Guard against stooping in old age by correcting your posture now and being sure that you get enough calcium.

Examine your weak points and be aware of how to correct them. Check your posture each and every day until it becomes a habit. Keep working and being aware of your good posture because it will do much to preserve your muscles and joints from the wear and tear of the advancing years.

A noted obstetrician said that if women would learn to correct their posture and let their organs sit where they should, there would be fewer female problems later in life.

Putting good posture rules into practice takes determination and a committed effort.

6

How Do You Sound Today?

The tongue that brings healing is a tree of life
—Proverbs 15:4

Your voice is one of the most important reflections of the real you that you can project to another person. It is important in all areas of your life whether you are just speaking in conversation or giving a speech. You can get the most expensive clothes, hairstyle, and makeup and really look like you are put together, but the way you speak will say a lot about you and the way you feel about yourself. Your voice should project authority, control, and confidence. Your voice should add to your image not subtract from it.

Speaking Beautifully

Sometimes you just need an awareness of how you sound to be able to begin to correct it. At least be aware of how you sound to others because it can cloud a whole picture of loveliness.

A voice that shows confidence is not too high nor too low, is not too loud nor too soft, is not a monotone but rather is distinct.

•

A lower pitched voice is easier to listen to than one that is too high. Consciously try to lower your voice so that your voice does not sound shrill.

•

Listen for any nasal sound as if you were talking through your nose. To test yourself to see if you sound nasal, pinch your nose and say Donald Duck. Then say it again without pinching. If you sound nasal, there will be little difference with the nose pinched or not.

•

Use a tape recorder and tape your telephone conversations and then play back the recording. This will help you to catch words like um, uh, you know, and other words you do not even realize you are saying. It will also give you an idea how many times you say them. This can be an annoying habit when these words are repeated too often.

If your voice sounds monotone,
try singing in the shower
to help with voice variety.

Another area to listen for is your pronunciation. Are you pronouncing words correctly or are you leaving the endings such as the "ings" off of your words?

•

Check your rate of speech. Are you speaking too quickly or too slowly and do you enunciate your words correctly?

•

If your voice sounds breathy, learn to take deep breaths that will fill your lungs. Practice reading a sentence without taking a breath.

•

To correct a shallow-sounding voice, try speaking from the diaphragm and use your lung power rather than just your mouth and throat.

•

Speak into the crease of a magazine to test your voice for tone quality.

•

When speaking, do you clear your throat constantly?

•

Do you slur over words?

•

Learning to relax when you speak is a big help. Especially relax the lips, tongue, and jaw.

———————— ✑ ————————

Try reading aloud to improve your voice.
Use poetry or prose and listen
to recordings of fine actors
and actresses who speak pleasantly.

Speaking in public can be one of your biggest fears and the only way to get over this fear is to know your material well, be confident of your voice, and practice over and over again until you realize that you can do a good job.

•

If you are serious about wanting to improve your oratory ability, it might be a good idea for you to take lessons from a voice teacher or join a club that will help you make speeches.

•

Practice speaking to small groups and then work up to larger ones. Even if you never have the goal of being a speaker, your voice still needs to be pleasant in ordinary conversation.

•

Allow warmth to come through in your speaking tone. This quality, plus an excitement and sparkle in your eyes will convey love to your audience. If you do this then you will be able to win them over and you will automatically make your speech more acceptable.

•

Use graceful body movements and a pleasant voice and you will present a pleasant image.

Conversation

The art of being a good conversationalist takes some practice and also some awareness. Being aware of other people and their needs will endear you to them. A good conversationalist does not take over the conversation when other people are speaking and does not use the word "I" too much in the process. Learning to communicate effectively requires being sensitive to the other person.

—— ❧ ——

The next time you are in the presence of someone who starts to gossip, change the subject immediately.

•

Idle talk and mischievous tattletales are hurtful to others. This is an easy trap to fall into when we are conversing with someone, so immediately counteract the negative by saying something positive about someone. Do you wonder what gossipers say about you when you are not there?

•

Be very aware of the people in your circle and make every effort to draw them into the conversation

•

It is impolite to whisper or giggle when someone else is speaking. This can apply to a larger audience as well as to someone teaching a Sunday school class.

•

We can learn to become a good conversationalist by talking to others at every opportunity. This includes the gas station attendant, clerks, and those people we come in contact with every day. The more we practice the easier it becomes

•

The best way to get someone to talk is to ask them questions about themselves.

•

Do not get in the habit of interrupting or finishing someone else's sentence.

•

Some people think that if they never say anything they will not put their foot in their mouth, but that type of person is boring.

•

Always establish eye contact but do not stare.

•

Be careful not to let emotions get out of hand in a conversation.

Listening

Listening is a discipline that requires concentration and endurance. Good conversationalists will be good listeners; they will not just hear the words but they will really hear what the person is saying.

———— ❧ ————

Learning to converse takes two, so a balance of talking and listening will make you more interesting.

•

Listen actively as others talk by keeping your eyes focused on the speaker so they will know that they have your complete attention.

•

When we actively listen to another person we get something from them and then respond to it. This completes the communication circuit which promotes understanding.

•

We usually are closest to and feel the most comfortable with people who listen well. There is a difference between being a good listener and just being polite when someone else is speaking without being really interested in what is said.

•

A good listener does not always think of a person's wealth or social status before she thinks she can learn something from that person. A good listener is someone flexible enough to enjoy the conversation of an eight-year-old child or the chairman of the board of a large corporation.

•

When a person is a good listener, he or she does not jump to any conclusions about the speaker.

7

Grooming Completes the Look

Then you will look and be radiant.
—Isaiah 60:5

One of the things that some women fail to take into consideration when dressing fashionably is their personal grooming. Personal grooming can be easily overlooked if one's lifestyle is very busy, but there is no way to look fashionable and successful if your grooming is not up to snuff. Let's go over some of the basics.

Clothes

Be sure your collar is free of dandruff. This is especially important when wearing dark-colored clothes. Take a soft, wet washcloth and brush the shoulder area before you step out.

•

Be sure the hem of your garment is sewn correctly and not pulled or puckered.

•

Be sure that your clothes are always free of wrinkles and spots. You can have the most beautiful wardrobe but if it is not kept clean and pressed it will look sloppy. Your dress or suit may be beautiful but if it is soiled, snagged, or stained, it will not flatter you, so treat your clothes to the best care you can give them on a regular basis. This will not only improve your image but will increase the shelf life of your clothes.

•

Check all buttons to be sure that they all match and that none are hanging.

•

White blouses and shirts should be worn only once because of hair oil on the collar and dirt on the cuffs. To remove hair oil, try rubbing shampoo on the collar ring instead of using detergent.

•

Do not carry sharp or heavy objects in your pockets because they can pull the fabric out of shape or even break the seams. Things that you carry in your pockets can wear out the linings more quickly, so store those things in your handbag.

•

Refuse to wear anything too tight, too low, too clingy, or too sheer.

•

Pay special attention to any hanging threads and be sure to remove all spots and perspiration stains. Job interviews or tense business meetings can be nerve-wracking and may call for special attention to body odor and underarm stains.

Stains

If you get something on your clothing, treat it as soon as possible. Rinse with water if the fabric is washable and the stain is water-soluble.

•

Be very careful with silk fabrics because in attempting to get out the stain, you can remove the color from the silk fabric.

•

Keep a bottle of special fabric spot remover for more difficult stains.

•

Always test your stain remover on your fabric in an inconspicuous place to prevent ruining your garment.

General Grooming Tips

Most people want to look as good as possible but it takes planning, organization, and awareness to accomplish this. Personal grooming is essential to give you that final polished look.

—— 🐝 ——

Take time to care for your hands and nails. This is an area that some women have a tendency to forget and it takes away from the total look.

•

Pantyhose with baggy knees and runs should be avoided. It is a good idea to have an extra pair in your handbag in case a run occurs. Never go without hosiery when dealing with the public.

•

Be sure that you look in a full-length mirror before going out so you can see if your slip or lining is hanging below the hem of your garment.

•

Be sure that your undergarment straps are not showing, or cannot be seen through sheer material. There are many beautiful camisoles to wear under sheer blouses. If straps are a problem, try sewing a small strapholder underneath. This works especially well on sleeveless dresses.

•

Be sure that you allow both deodorants and perfumes to dry thoroughly before putting on your clothes. These products can discolor or even weaken certain fabrics.

•

Do not wear excessive or cheap perfume. No perfume may be better than too much, especially if you work in close quarters with others.

•

Never forget your underarm deodorant.

•

Be aware of your breath and keep breath mints on hand. Do not chew gum. Gum-chewing takes away from the femininity of a woman.

•

Take good care of your teeth through regular visits to the dentist. Many breath problems come from rotting teeth and unhealthy gums. Your teeth should be brushed frequently and cleaned professionally to prevent yellowing.

•

Do not wear jewelry that will pull a thread on the fabric of your outfit.

•

Remove your shoes before stepping in and out of skirts and pants to prevent catching the hem with the heel or toe of your shoe.

•

If you get dressed after you have put your makeup on, take a scarf and hold one corner with your teeth. Then put it over the top of your hair and tie at the neck. This will prevent makeup from getting on any clothing you may put over your head.

•

If you put your makeup on after you get dressed, put on a dress shield or drape a towel over your shoulders to protect your clothing.

•

Be aware of any holes in the back of your hairdo.

•

Remember, people see you from the back as well as the front so check your heels and the tips of your shoes. Run-down heels and scuffed, dirty shoes are not the look of success.

PART 2

Beauty Basics

8

Put On Your Best Face— Makeup and Skin Care

Wisdom brightens a man's face and changes its hard appearance.
—Ecclesiastes 8:1

General Skin Care

When you do not drink enough water, your body will take water from your skin and cause it to become dry. To prevent this from happening, drink at least six to eight glasses of water a day. Juice or other drinks are not included. This practice is good for the whole body because it will cleanse your system and remove toxins. When the outer layer of skin contains adequate water, it plumps up and looks smoother.

Skin renews itself every 28 days, so begin a healthy program today and in about a month there should be marked improvement. Though makeup is optional, skin care is a must for every woman Without a good skin-care program, your makeup will not be as effective

It is easier than you think to set up a beautification program. Once you learn what you need to do and get it set up, it becomes as automatic as brushing your teeth.

The general health of the body is reflected in the skin. Stress causes the glands to secrete oil rapidly and in spurts and then blemishes begin to pop up. A hit-and-miss beauty program will not work, so make consistency one of your goals and it will bring you rewards. Heredity may offer an advantage but it is up to you to do the rest

Cleansing

——— ॐ ———

Remove makeup thoroughly. Neglect in this area is one of the major causes of skin problems. Use as much time taking makeup off as you do putting it on. If you leave dirt behind on your face, it will cause your skin to look dull, which can make you look older. Check to see that there are no traces of soap or makeup left when you are finished. A clean face is imperative to healthy-looking skin.

•

Pay particular attention to the areas around the nose, mouth, and eyes. When removing makeup, use a soft cloth or cotton balls. Never use tissues because paper fibers are rough on the skin.

•

Always remove your makeup before you go to bed. If you do not do this, your skin will pay for it later.

•

You can improve circulation with surface masks and granular scrubs.

•

It is important to maintain the pH balance of your skin. Soaps that have a high pH upset the natural chemical balance, strip the skin of its normal protection, and dry the skin. Soaps like this should be avoided.

•

Do not wash your face with hot water and harsh soaps; instead use a cleansing bar or cleansing creams

•

Always rub your face gently when applying or removing makeup or a mask. If you rub harshly or pull downward it can be damaging to your skin. Rough rubbing or strong products used on the skin can make fine lines and wrinkles more noticeable.

•

Light circular motions are best when cleansing the skin.

•

Be sure that your hair is pulled back when you cleanse your face so that you can effectively remove oil on the jawline and hairline.

•

Eyes need special attention because the skin around the eyes is very delicate and can be pulled too tightly when cleansing. If pulled and pushed every day, this skin may have a tendency to sag. Be very gentle in this area.

•

Get in the habit of using a good cleansing mask.

•

Creams that have cleansing grains in them which take away the top layer of dead skin cells can help your complexion look fresher and brighter.

A sponge that has an abrasive material on it for removing dead cells should be used with a soft touch.

Stay away from astringents with a lot of alcohol.

Moisturizing

Choose a water-based moisturizer regardless of your skin type.

•

A wrinkle stick used around the eyes and mouth two or three times a day helps refresh your moisturizer.

•

A good moisturizer will help trap water in your skin.

•

To help your moisturizer work more effectively, try applying it when your face is still a little damp after cleansing.

•

Neglecting a good skin-care program will show up first on your neck and hands. Start moisturizing when you are young to get a head start on slowing the aging process.

•

Your oil gland output slows down after age 25 and then slows even more before menopause so as you age you should increase your use of moisturizers in your skin-care regimen.

Tips for Healthy Skin

———— ❧ ————

For a lasting glow, try exercise. It promotes good circulation which increases the flow of nourishing blood and oxygen to your skin. Exercise gives circulation a big boost and helps fight stress which relaxes all body muscles including those of the face. Whatever benefits the body will benefit the skin.

•

Do not do a lot of crash dieting; it will show up on the skin.

•

Smog is another cause of early wrinkles and lifeless skin.

•

Regardless of your age, start your skin-care program now. Also, don't think that just because you are young you do not need a good skin-care program.

•

Take some breaks during your day to save you from too much tension that is bound to show up in your skin.

•

One good way to avoid facial wrinkles is to sleep on your back. If you must use a pillow, use it under the back of your neck so that it doesn't push lines into your face.

Habits Affecting Skin

Improper food, drinking, smoking, and late hours will produce flaws in figures and on faces much earlier than normal. Alcohol and cigarettes are very bad for the skin.

Alcohol dilates the blood vessels and leads to blotching. Smoking is linked to premature wrinkles because it is known to deplete vitamin C, which is essential to forming skin-supporting collagen. Also creases around the eyes and mouth may be accentuated by puffing and squinting through a haze of smoke. Give up smoking not only for your health but also for your skin's sake.

Diet

—— 🙠 ——

A wholesome eating plan that makes you healthy is essential for the best complexion. Eat lots of vegetables and fruits and less sugar.

•

One of the worst things that you can do to your skin is to yo-yo diet. The continual losing and gaining of weight can stretch the skin, accentuate wrinkles, break down the supporting skin fibers, and make you look older.

•

Other ways to take good care of your skin are to avoid too much salt, sugar, and caffeine.

•

Some of the most important vitamins and minerals for a healthy complexion are the B vitamins, and vitamins A and C. Eat beef, chicken, whole wheat breads, milk, green leafy vegetables, carrots, and fresh fruit to get the best supply of these important vitamins and minerals.

Makeup Tips

Makeup should not be a coverup but instead should be a device to bring out your natural beauty. Makeup is like a wardrobe for your face just as clothing is for your body.

It is as important to look attractive and wear attractive attire around the house for your spouse as it is when you go out. It contributes to good morale when you look your best and it makes your spouse feel he is important.

—— 🙠 ——

If you do not know where to start in a makeup program, go to a reputable cosmetologist and let her help you get started.

•

Blending is the key to keep makeup soft, so use sponges and brushes for blending. This will help your makeup look more natural.

•

Clean your makeup tools in warm sudsy water when you are done using them to prevent harmful bacteria from getting in your eyes and on your skin.

•

Choose a mascara that goes on smoothly without clumping on your lashes.

---

*Wear makeup
a little lighter in the daytime
and a little darker at night.*

If you wear contacts, use fragrance-free eye makeup, especially mascara. Also, look for makeup without metallic flakes that may get into the eyes.

•

Check out your makeup techniques by examining your face in natural light and looking at the total effect. Blend any hard lines with a soft sponge.

•

In the morning, if you will apply your foundation and eyeshadow before getting into the bath or shower, the moisture will help to set these bases and keep your makeup looking fresher longer.

•

Oil-based makeup can enlarge your pores. Water-based makeup is better.

•

Always take time to smudge your eyeliner with your finger, edge of the applicator, or a Q-tip so that you do not have a harsh black or blue line on your eye.

•

Makeup under eyeglasses looks good but you may have to add a bit more. However, if the lenses are magnified then the makeup can look a little exaggerated or too harsh under the eyeglasses. Experiment and check the look in natural light.

•

If you use bright blue or green eye shadows and they are not completely blended, they will mask the color of your eyes. Blues and greens are very difficult to blend so that they look natural as eye shadow should. You should not look at someone and see two green or blue eyelids going up and down. If you do use these colors, try combining them with charcoal grays or browns which will at least tone them down and help neutralize them.

•

Mauves and taupes for cool-skinned people and earth tones for warm-skinned people have proven to be nice shadows to use.

•

When applying eye makeup, if you have protruding or puffy eyes, use darker shades and avoid light or frosted colors.

•

Apply foundation to lids first for easier shadow application. To prevent eye makeup from running or creasing, dust powder on lids and brow before applying shadow and only use powder shadow.

•

Do not let your makeup get too old because it can harbor bacteria. It is best to replace your mascara after three to four months.

•

Be careful when using tester cosmetics at department stores. They can spread some infections to the mouth and face if you do not use precautions.

———

Becoming more attractive is like almost anything else; it is a step-by-step process. Don't be bound by what you have decided are your limitations.

Lipstick

If you use a lip liner, it will help keep your lipstick from running out of the line and into the creases on your upper lip. Be careful that this liner is blended into the lipstick so that no line shows. You can use a lip liner to improve an irregular lip shape. Some of the experts in cosmetics extend a thin lip line to make it look fuller but if you attempt to do this, be sure it is done properly. Generally speaking, do not try to extend lipstick out of the natural lip line. The best way to apply lipstick is to use a lip-liner brush first, then fill in with a lipstick brush, blot with a tissue, and seal with powder for staying power.

If you know your color key and use it to coordinate your wardrobe, you will not need as many cosmetics or lipsticks. If you are a cool-skinned person your cool shades will go with everything that you wear. The same is true for warm-skinned people.

To choose the right lipstick, take a good look at your lips.

—— ❧ ——

Thin lips: Try a light lipstick and then apply a gloss over the center of your mouth to highlight the fullest area. If you have a small mouth, use lighter, glossier shades of lipstick to enlarge your lips.

•

Full lips: Wear darker shades of a low luster lipstick and apply more lipstick on the bottom lip. Try to avoid calling too much attention to your mouth with bright lip colors.

•

Uneven lips: Try to equalize them by using a dark lipstick on your lower lip and then the next lighter shade available on your upper lip. Once again, lip liner helps here also. To find lip colors that work together, check the numbers on the lipsticks or color charts. The two shades of lipstick should be close in color value so no one will notice an obvious difference between your upper and lower lips.

•

To extend a lip that seems to be a bit droopy, outline the lower lip slightly upward.

•

Lipstick is a protector and even if you do not wear a color, you should wear a clear lipstick to protect your lips from the sun, wind, and cold.

•

Your best lip colors are the ones that suit your color's season. Warm springs or autumns should use peach, tawny, coral, rust, and orange reds. Cool summers and winters should use rosy pinks, plums, mauves, and blue reds.

Be aware that not all lipstick colors look the same on all women.

Creamy lipsticks have a higher oil content, give a glossier look to lips, and are softer than the no-smear types.

•

Powder your mouth lightly with translucent powder if you have a problem with your lipstick developing fuzzy edges or not lasting.

•

Younger women and young girls look best in the glossy lipsticks.

•

Lip glosses or gels are best applied with the fingertips.

•

If you want the gloss to last longer, then use a cream lipstick as a base coat.

•

One problem is that lipstick may change color on our lips. If it does, perhaps your body chemistry is causing the problem. To prevent this put a primer coat of foundation on your lips before applying lip color.

The experts say that the dyes in lipstick are not absorbed by our lips because the skin on the lips is similar to that on the palms of our hands and soles of our feet and it has very few pores.

Blush

To keep powder blush from streaking over moisturizer, use the dry-on-dry principle. When applying blush, apply moist blush to foundation, then put on a translucent powder and reapply powder blush over the powder. If you try to put a powder blush directly onto your cream foundation, it will blotch. Remember in applying blush, cream goes on cream, powder on powder.

Blush is one of the most important things that a woman can apply to her face to give her that healthy glow, or it can be the most obvious mistake when applied as two little round apple cheeks.

—— 🐛 ——

Your blush color and lip color should be in the same color family.

•

You cannot judge the darkness or lightness of a color by the name given to it. Try it on before you decide. Sometimes a blush color that looks too deep will blend out to a healthy glow on your skin.

•

If you choose a blush shade that is too light it will just sit on your cheek and look artificial.

•

Darker skins need a richer, brighter blush color.

•

Powder blush produces a soft matte finish and is easy to brush on when your makeup needs a touch-up during the day.

•

Put your blush on softly, starting from the outside corner of your temple and stroking in a wedge on the cheekbone.

•

When applying blush, stroke upward.

●

Do not apply the color too close to the eyes or too close to the nose. If you do this, it will make the eyes look smaller and will close up the face. A good guide is to place your index finger alongside your nose and bring your cheek color no closer to your nose than the outer edge of your finger.

●

Do not bring the blush down too far on your face for this will make you look drawn. Stop at a point even with or slightly above the bottom of your nose.

●

To blend cream blush, always tap with fingertips or a damp makeup sponge. Be sure it is well blended on the edges. Do not rub or pull at your skin.

Eyes

Your eyes are very important and should not be neglected. Relaxation, good circulation, and proper nutrition add to your eye health. Coffee, tea, and smoking all constrict the blood vessels. Vitamins B, C, and A are all essential to good eye health.

——— ?● ———

Many people think that crow's feet that develop around the eyes are hereditary but the fact is, you do not have to have them. They are usually the result of poor vision habits, squinting, and neglect of the skin in the eye area.

●

One of the best tricks for making your eyes look less tired during the day and for adding a more glowing complexion is applying some blush to your cheeks with a brush.

●

The skin around your eyes needs special pampering by applying rich eye creams or moisturizers at night or whenever you are out in the sun for a long time. Do not rub it in but pat it around the eye gently from the outer corner to the inner corner.

●

It's a good idea to wear a brimmed hat that shades your eyes or wear dark glasses to keep from squinting when you are in the sun.

•

Take periodic eye breaks when your eye muscles get tired. Try shifting the focus of your gaze to distant objects around the room for a few seconds. Open and close your eyes four or five times very rapidly.

Make sure that the lighting in your home or office is not too bright or too dull.

Eye exercises can help to strengthen your eye muscles. Try placing your head against the wall so your head will not move. Look high at one corner of the room and then move your eyes slowly from one corner to the other, left to right and then right to left.

•

Some studies have shown that writing with red ink for long periods of time can cause eyestrain and headaches.

•

As you get older, your eyes need even more protection, so do not let the ultraviolet rays of the sun cause retinal damage or cataracts. A good pair of sunglasses would be a good investment.

Circles Under the Eyes

The area under the eye does not contain oil glands and is very prone to wrinkling, dark circles, lines, redness, and puffiness or a combination of two or more of these problems.

——— 🙐 ———

Try to get an adequate amount of sleep. However, too much sleep can sometimes cause circles under the eyes.

•

Use a good highlighter cream. It should be lighter than your foundation and your complexion.

•

There are some good stick concealers that could also be used before applying the foundation.

•

Blend outward and upward.

•

Apply foundation over the highlighter under the eye.

•

Keep a light touch avoid a heavy look.

•

Moles, birthmarks, pimples, and other blemishes usually can be effectively covered using the same basic concealing techniques that are used to cover under-eye circles and dark spots.

Puffiness Under the Eyes

——— 🙐 ———

Do not put highlighter directly on the puffy area because the lighter shade will tend to make the area more prominent.

•

Darker shades make an area recede so it would be best to apply concealer in the shadow under and around the puffiness.

Makeup for the Summer Months and Skin Care in the Sun

Warm summer months require different beauty priorities. Heat becomes the biggest problem to cope with instead of dryness and cold. Hot sun is very drying to skin and hair, so moisturize frequently. Moisturizers are important during the spring and summer but for different reasons than when used in the winter.

—— 🐛 ——

Increase your intake of water.

•

Powder can be a useful makeup tool during the hot summer months. Baby powder sprinkled on the body can help keep you nice and cool.

•

Translucent powders for the face work well for removing shininess and for adding more of a matte finish.

•

To add an extra glow to your makeup, brush your blush on your cheeks and then give an extra fluff of blush to your forehead, near your hairline, and on the tip of your chin.

•

Powder makeup is good all summer because it will absorb oil better and lessen the chances of creasing or perspiring off.

•

Powder blush will stay on better in hot weather. Use it over your translucent powder.

•

There are powder-type eye pencils for those who wish to experiment with the new summer looks.

•

Hot weather can sometimes lead to puffiness around the eyes. Try a couple of slices of cool cucumber on the eyes for a soothing effect. You can feel it work. Slices of raw potato can also help reduce puffiness.

•

If the sun has dried your lips and caused some tiny creases around your mouth, avoid greasy lipsticks because they will have a tendency to spread into these furrows.

•

Choose a lipstick that will stay on when swimming. This will also help keep your lips from getting irritated from the sun, perspiration, and water.

•

If your lips are very dry, do not go outdoors with them unprotected. Wear lipstick, gloss, or a lip balm. When you wear lipstick, it lessens the chance of chapping because it is a protector and seals in the lips' natural moisture. When this natural moisture evaporates from sun, wind, heat, or dry climate, your lips can become sensitive, irritated, cracked and they can even bleed, so keep them adequately protected.

----

*Don't forget to give your neck
the same care that you give your face.*

Daylight in summer is especially intense so be sure to avoid shiny and frosted lipsticks which can look artificial in bright light. It is better to use a lipstick that leaves a more natural-looking finish. Use some softer shades such as coral for a warm-skinned woman and the soft roses and pinks for the cool-skinned woman.

•

In the summer, switch to a light, water-based foundation to avoid a shiny look on your face.

Tanning

You have heard it said repeatedly that the sun is your worst enemy for aging your skin. Sun affects the different skin types in different ways. For instance, blonds and redheads are the most likely to be sun sensitive and will burn faster than those with darker complexions. A darker skin has a protective pigment that works like a shield against the sun. But whoever you are, the effects of too much sun will be a thickened and weathered skin texture with premature wrinkles.

—— ❧ ——

If you have already gotten an overdose of sun, it is not too late to use a sunscreen every day and in every season so you can stop the damage and even help your skin to heal itself. However, they say, "Once a wrinkle always a wrinkle."

•

Suntan slowly by starting with ten minutes a day and then increase that five minutes each day, working up gradually from there. Do not wait until you see red before you cover up. Do not try to acquire a tan in a day or a weekend. Take the sun in small doses.

•

If you get a tan, the foundation you normally use may not match as well. Use a new foundation that matches the changes in your skin.

—— ❧ ——

Be aware that if you have burned once, it will make you more susceptible to another bad burn.

•

You can wear eye shadows that are a little brighter when you have a tan.

•

If you have been burned badly enough to blister or if your skin becomes swollen, see a doctor.

•

When you are near water the extra reflection of the sun requires extra protection. This is true of overcast days as well.

•

Take a hat to further protect your face.

•

Remember in hot weather you must moisturize not only on the outside but also from the inside. Drink plenty of fluids to replenish what is lost through perspiration.

•

Also eat fruits and vegetables daily because they are very good for the skin.

•

To reduce peeling, moisturize all over with a rich lotion. Do not overlook moisturizing the back of your knees, tops of your feet, elbows, ears, and your neck.

•

The sun is the most intense between 11 A.M. and 3 P.M. so be very careful during this time.

•

Do not forget that you can burn while swimming because the sun rays go right through the water, so count the time swimming as time sunning.

•

At the beach, the sun can bounce off the sand and right under an umbrella or hat.

•

Snow is one of the worst culprits, bouncing back up to 85 percent of the sun's burning rays.

•

Don't be fooled by haze and fog because it will still allow ultraviolet light through and give a memorable burn.

•

Take the sting out of a sunburn by soaking in a tub filled with lukewarm water and three or four tea bags. The tannic acid can be very soothing

Suntan Lotions and Protectors

Sun protection factor (SPF) lotions which are between 2 and 30 indicate how much protection you will get from the sunscreen. The higher the number, the more protection. For instance, if you could stay in the sun for 15 minutes without burning, then with a sunscreen that has a sun protection factor of 2 you would be able to stay out twice as long or 30 minutes without burning. Get a good sunblock with an SPF of at least 15. Apply the sunblock whenever sunbathing or whenever you're around the water.

—— 〜 ——

Apply sunscreen evenly, and always reapply after swimming.

•

Pay special attention to hot spots like the nose, cheeks, knees, and lips because they are often forgotten in the sun and they can get really burned.

•

If suntan lotions do not work for you, perhaps you are not using them properly. The lotion needs to be applied and reapplied while you are exposed to the sun. One time usually doesn't do it. Perspiration and going into the water will remove some protection.

•

If you get swollen, sunburned lips, use special care around the mouth. There are special sunstick lip protectors and lip balms on the market.

•

Eye shadows are good protection against burned eyelids. Powder shadows are best in summer and do not get soft and run on your lids.

Cold Weather Tips
—— 〜 ——

Though cold, crisp winter air is invigorating, it is hard on the skin. Strong winds and low humidity deplete the skin of moisture and leave it dry, flaky, or scaly. Sometimes when the office or home is too hot, which makes the humidity low, it can have the same effect.

•

Be careful of the kind of soap that you use and choose one suited to your skin type. Do not use soap on your face unless it is a specially-made soap for faces.

•

If your skin is very dry, use a cream cleanser. Add some baby oil to your bathwater.

•

For the greatest benefit, moisturize your face and body immediately after bathing while you are still damp. The moisturizer will help trap water in your skin.

•

A humidifier at home or in the office can help with dry skin problems. If you do not have one try boiling some water on your stove this will give off some humidity.

The Bath

If you have always been the no-nonsense type of person who hurries up and takes a shower, you owe it to yourself to experience the tranquil pleasures of a bath. Health spas have long relied on the magic of water mixed with herbs, mud, and the essential oils of plants or mineral salts to smooth skin, refine pores, relax tense muscles, and help our bodies feel rejuvenated. Many European hydrotherapists use water as a healing agent for everything from minor colds to pneumonia.

Most people take baths that are too hot. Frequent hot bathing can have a loosening effect on muscles and skin and can cause skin to age. The temperature of a bath should be a warm 85 to 95 degrees. A cool bath is more stimulating and a tepid bath before bedtime will help you sleep. Hot water is not good for you because it dries and ages your skin and may even injure delicate capillaries and veins.

——— 🐌 ———

Before your bath light a few candles around the room to create a relaxing atmosphere.

•

Put some of your favorite scent into the tub and let it make the air fragrant.

•

A great beauty aid is a dry, rough-textured loofah sponge that you soften by wetting. Rub it against your skin to slough off dead cells and increase circulation. This is especially helpful for that dry skin on your heels.

•

A massage before you bathe is good for very dry skin.

•

If you put a little baby oil into the bath with a few drops of your favorite cologne or perfume, the scent will cling to your body.

•

Splash water onto your face and let it soak in while you bathe.

•

Taking a cool bath for no longer than ten minutes will give you a refreshing start.

•

If you have a hard time waking up in the morning, shower with warm water and slowly turn the water down to a cooler temperature. Breathe deeply in the shower as you let your whole body relax by dangling your arms and head. Let the shower beat on the nape of your neck, shoulders, and back; these are the key tension spots.

Focus on Your Good Points

Study women who you think are attractive and figure out what it is that pleases your eye. Is it the way that they wear their makeup or their hairstyle, or is it something elusive like the way that they speak and gesture?

Sometimes people do not see themselves as they are and therefore cannot make the right changes or even discern good advice when they hear it. Do not get obsessed with your faults and do not blow them out of proportion but concentrate on your positive attributes and capitalize on them.

Many women who have been known as beautiful did not always have perfect features. Oftentimes their beauty reputation was earned from their warmth, sympathy, and interest in others. Beauty should not be an overconsuming thing but instead should be a means to an end. Some of the top models are not that beautiful. They work at analyzing themselves and they learn to emphasize their best assets and de-emphasize their less-than-perfect parts.

CHAPTER

9

Help with Hair

*Indeed the very hairs of your head
are all numbered.*
—Luke 12:7

Your hair should be one of the most positive impressions that you make. Not only is it one of the first things that people notice about you but it also offers you the most immediate area of change to improve your image. The way that you wear your hair, the color you put on it, and the kind of condition it is in, all reflect a style and indicate a definite statement about you. If you will step out and experiment with color and style, you can create a whole new look; one that will perhaps takes years off your age. If a person's hair does not look good, other things do not seem to matter.

Nutrition for the Hair

Nutrition for the hair is very important. Since your hair is actually old protein, nutritionists say it cannot receive nourishment from vitamins in any hair care products. There are varied opinions on this because some companies say they can put protein into the hair, but unless you have a good balance of protein in your diet, your hair will not have the glow of health. If your diet does not include a wide variety of nutrients from which your hair can feed, no amount of hair care techniques will help. Hair and nails can be a real barometer of your health. Sometimes when hair falls out, there is a thyroid deficiency.

Nutritionists say that fish is brain food but it is also hair food. This is because fish are full of minerals and zinc which makes for healthy and shining hair. A good balanced diet including vitamins and minerals will help maintain growth of strong, healthy-looking hair.

Shampoo

How often you shampoo varies with the type of hair and scalp you have, your hairstyle, and personal preference. Since your hair takes a lot of abuse from styling, blow drying, and overheated rooms, the use of creme rinses or deep conditioners can improve the feel and texture of your hair.

—— 🍃 ——

Hair should be squeaky clean at all times.

•

Wash your hair as often as you need to and do not worry about washing it too much. A mild shampoo should clean quickly and efficiently.

•

Choose a shampoo that does not contain paraben as it will coat the hair and eventually keep it from curling. Many shampoos may coat the hair so ask your hairdresser to recommend a good one. Companies that specialize and do research on hair care products will usually have good shampoos and conditioners.

•

Treat your hair as gently as possible after washing by squeezing out the excess water and not rubbing vigorously.

•

Use conditioners frequently and occasionally use a moisturizing treatment if your hair is very dry. Products recommended for your specific hair type and problem areas are always the best to use. If you do not know what your hair needs, then consult with a reputable hairdresser, tell her your specific problem, and she will tell you what to do.

Dandruff

A healthy scalp is very important to a healthy head of hair. Do not automatically assume that a scaling scalp means that you have permanent dandruff because this problem could be caused by several things.

———— 🍂 ————

Dandruff can be caused by a sunburned scalp.

•

The use of certain hair sprays or setting lotions can dry the scalp and hair. Leave hairspray and setting lotions off your hair for a week or two and see if it helps.

•

Before you switch to a dandruff shampoo, give your regular shampoo a chance to work by rinsing it out more thoroughly.

•

Treat dry scalp with a light oil massage.

Hairstyle and Face Shape

A competent hairdresser is a must in getting a cut that not only can be easily styled but will also fit your face shape. A good way to find out your face shape is to stand in front of a mirror and draw the outline of your face onto the mirror with a lipstick or bar of soap. This will give you a pretty good idea where you are wide and narrow.

———— 🍂 ————

A round face needs hair feathered forward to the chin. This softness slims the roundness.

•

The long, angular, rectangular face can be shortened if you swirl bangs from the crown and taper hair to the chin. Do not wear hair straight down on the sides.

•

The square face needs some feather bangs that wave to the temples and a soft pageboy at the jawline.

•

Diamond faces need width at the jawline and soft bangs to give the illusion of a broader forehead.

•

The pear-shaped face needs to add volume and fullness at the temples with a soft, fuller, more curly style.

•

Heart-shaped faces should keep hair close to the crown and temple to de-emphasize the fullness of the forehead and cheekbones. Add softness and fullness at the chinline.

•

The perfectly-shaped face is the oval and you can wear your hair in almost any style.

•

During the warm months, have your hair trimmed more frequently than usual. Hair grows faster in the summer and exposure to the elements of summer causes split ends.

Hair Color

The right hair color can brighten your whole face, flatter your skin tones, light up your eyes, and bring out your personality. Softer, lighter hair colors tend to project a friendlier image. Too dark a hair color can create a stern look. Any color change in your hair, whether it is a subtle or dramatic change, depends on your own natural hair color plus your skin tone. Here is another good reason to know whether your color key is cool or warm.

——— 𝜗 ———

Start with the color you have. If it is mousy or drab, add a few highlights to give it a sunny look or color your hair a little lighter.

•

A good way to find out what you will look like in certain colors is to try on some wigs.

•

Warm hair colors will seem to stand out more to an observer. A good example is a redhead.

•

Cool hair colors, the ashen hair colors or those with no reddish or golden undertones, will not stand out as much.

•

If your face is too round, it can look slimmer by using a side part and by adding color highlights on the top.

•

A too-thin face can be made to look broader by adding fullness at the sides and a hair color lighter than your own.

•

Facial features that look too sharp can be softened with a curly hairstyle and a lighter hair color.

•

To make deep-set eyes appear larger and wider, pull the hair toward the face at the forehead and add some blond highlights at the temples.

•

If your forehead is too high, cover it with bangs and highlight your hair from your crown to the tips of your bangs and the sides to play up your eyes.

•

If you have never colored or lightened your hair, take it easy because too little is better than too much.

Gray Hair

Gray hair can be beautiful and very attractive. There is no scientific evidence to say that stress causes gray hair. Gray hair most often occurs as a natural part of the aging process and heredity plays a very important role in determining when and how quickly this process occurs.

Some of the other causes of gray hair are a metabolic upset, nervous system problem, endocrine gland disorder, physical or mental shock, or severe illness.

Graying because of age is irreversible; however if the graying results from other causes, color may come back to the hair when the person recovers from the illness.

General Hair Care Tips

Hair is said to grow faster between the ages of 15 and 25 Cutting the hair does not affect the hair growth, although removing the split ends improves the appearance. Hair grows on the average of one-quarter to one-half inch every month

—— ❧ ——

Never wear curlers in public. It does not make a good first impression.

•

The first way to stop hair abuse is to stop using the wrong products. Treat your hair gently. Your hair will survive a certain amount of abuse but if you want beautiful hair, the key word is care. Beautiful hair is essential to good grooming.

•

Everyday blow drying or hot roller styling will also abuse your hair and dry it out.

•

Be careful when you choose hair ornaments and hair fasteners because sharp edges on barrettes and uncoated plastic will break your hair.

---

*Make sure that you brush your hair
every day to remove all traces
of styling products and hair spray.*

Make sure that you are brushing your hair with the right brush. Wide-set plastic bristles fluff the hair and are best for adding lift and volume to any style. Thicker, denser bristles, either natural or nylon, will smooth hair.

•

Sometimes the hair will become more manageable when using some good gels and lotions. Using too much, however, can leave the hair sticky and difficult to manage and style.

•

We work at hair level when styling our hair but the hairdresser works from above and hair is a lot easier to guide and manage from that angle. So raise your arms above your head and reach down to style your hair.

•

Put peanut butter on your fingers and rub it into your hair to remove chewing gum. The gum should come loose and then you will need to wash as usual.

Perms

It is best not to attempt complicated chemical processing of the hair at home. You may end up spending more in the end to have a professional correct your mistakes than you would having it done right in the first place. Get a professional perm which will enable you greater styling freedom with little or no trouble. Many women fight with their hair all their lives because they are afraid to get a permanent, but a good perm will build body in your hair. Today, perms have been improved to give you curls or just a body wave, and they even have spot perms. Have your hair in really good condition first. Be sure you go to a reputable hairdresser.

Sometimes before a permanent can be given, the hair needs to be stripped to get the buildup of hair products off of the hair. Commercial stripping products are best for this problem. If you do not get the buildup off of your hair before you perm, it may not curl. Your hairdresser can advise you on this.

After you perm, get frequent trims to snip off any split ends.

Styling

The biggest help in taking care of your hair is to get it cut correctly for your hair texture and your face shape. Hair that is all different lengths and going every which way makes the grow-out time harder than it needs to be. Even if you just have a little length removed, your hair will look better and be easier to manage.

——— 🌿 ———

Use some fashionable barrettes to keep your hair out of the way and give it a sleek, more pulled-together appearance.

•

To get volume in your hair, use a soft hair spray and spray the hair thoroughly, brushing the spray through the hair for even distribution. Allow the spray to dry for a few minutes and then bend over and brush the hair down for volume. Stand up and shake the hair into place and then brush lightly again.

•

If your hair gets wilted in the hot humid weather, try pulling the sides of your hair back with some beautiful combs or change your part to the other side to give yourself a fuller look.

Dull Hair

Healthy hair shines because it reflects light. If your hair is in good condition, light will be reflected; however, if your hair is damaged, light will be scattered and the overall look will be dull. Darker hair reflects light more than lighter hair, so people with black hair will seem to have shinier hair than blonds.

—— 🍃 ——

If your hair loses its shine when you are exercising vigorously, the culprit is probably perspiration, so wash it out frequently.

•

Overprocessing can also dull the hair.

•

Overexposure to sunlight which bleaches and dries out hair can cause your hair to look dull. So always wear a hat or scarf when you are out in the sun a long time.

•

Do not forget to protect your hair when you are swimming because chlorine attacks the protein in the hair and salt water can be very drying. Tucking your hair under a swimming cap may be a good idea.

•

If there is low humidity, it will make your hair dull because it saps the moisture from the hair and makes it more dry. Always use a good moisturizer for your hair if you live in a dry climate and especially during hot summer months.

•

The use of hard water can dull the hair because minerals may combine with the shampoo and leave a residue. If you have this problem use a good acidic rinse. You can make this yourself by mixing one-half cup of apple cider vinegar with four cups of water.

•

Pollution in the air can make hair dull and the solution is to shampoo more often.

•

If you have been sick or unusually stressed, your sebaceous glands produce more oil and this can cause dust and dirt to collect on the hair more readily, making it dull and limp. Use a shampoo for oily hair at this time.

•

It will only take a matter of weeks for a poor diet to show up in your hair. Remember, protein is a major component of hair and a poor diet will cause the hair to lack luster.

A Few Natural Hair Tips

Here are a few natural hair tips for those who do not want to spend a lot of money on manufactured hair care products.

——— 🐚 ———

Use baking soda on the scalp to blot up excess oils, brush to remove the granules of powder, and then rub down with a dry towel to restore shine.

———————————— 🐚 ————————————

Between shampoos,
sprinkle cornmeal in the hair to
loosen dust particles and then brush out.

To enhance body and luster to hair, mix a raw egg with a normal amount of shampoo needed to suds the hair. Lather as usual but be sure to rinse with cold water.

•

Other natural ingredients known to add shine to the hair are white vinegar rinses, lemon juice, or witch hazel. Two or three tablespoons of one of these items can be mixed with at least a quart of warm water and used as a final rinse. Be sure to rinse thoroughly.

•

Brewed tea rinses are said to bring out the natural highlights and are easy to make. The teas to use are camomile or marigold buds and they work well on hair of all colors. Brews made from shelled walnuts or sliced beets are for brunettes only.

•

Excellent hair conditioners are mayonnaise and oils such as olive, sesame, soybean, and safflower. Mayonnaise may be cool or at room temperature but the oils should be warmed before applying. After shampooing and rinsing, towel dry your hair to get rid of excess moisture and use enough mayonnaise or oil to completely coat your hair. Work it in with your fingers and then wrap your head in a plastic wrap to retain body heat which helps the oil penetrate for about 20 minutes. Shampoo and rinse thoroughly.

•

Natural products can be beneficial to your hair, but the most important ingredients are physical and emotional health.

Hair Loss

Losing hair is a very traumatic thing for both men and women. As we age, some decrease in hair count is perfectly normal. If you continue to lose your hair over weeks and months with no apparent regrowth, see your doctor and have some thyroid function tests.

Two of the reasons that women experience hair loss after the age of 40 are hormones and heredity. Some women and many men are born with a gene that lends itself toward baldness.

Men who lose hair seem to see the front hairline recede until only a horseshoe rim of hair remains over the ears and around the back of the head. A woman however, tends to retain the front hairline while the hair on the crown may get very thin. Hairs that remain on her head are smaller in diameter than they once were and grow at a slower rate, and usually she will not become totally bald as a man does.

———— ❧ ————

Try to lessen your stress level because temporary hair loss may be traced to stress in many cases. Once the stress is relieved, the hormonal balance is restored and normal hair growth can resume.

•

Other causes could be a major surgery or a long illness, an infection with a high fever, or a period of prolonged stress. Any of these causes can be temporary.

•

Also some medications can lead to thinning of the hair.

•

Another cause could be tight braids or ponytails.

Sometimes following a fad diet will increase hair loss, especially a diet that restricts protein.

Permanent hair loss from follicle destruction can result from prolonged pulling on the hair. It is best not to use tight curlers, clips, hairpins, or stiff hairbrushes.

•

Average amounts of hair processing, coloring, and permanents don't affect hair growth or loss. But women who do these processes too frequently will accelerate the tendency to temporarily thin hair on top.

•

A soft natural-bristle brush is the best brush and easiest on your hair.

•

If your hair is thinning, a wide-tooth comb with smooth, rounded ends would be better for your hair than a brush.

•

Intensive programs of exercise and scalp massage have never been shown to be a help in growing your hair back; however, what has been shown is that a too vigorous scalp massage can contribute to hair loss because of hair abuse. The basic rule that doctors do agree on is to be as gentle as possible with your hair.

CHAPTER

10

My, You Smell Good!
—Fragrances

Perfume and incense bring joy to the heart.
—Proverbs 27:9

Your personality will cause you to lean toward certain fragrances. For example, extroverts may choose something more wild than introverts. Many times we are attracted to someone because of the way she or he smells so never underestimate the power of scent. Wearing a good-quality fragrance can affect your mood.

There was a study done by a large fragrance firm and they found that a person's fragrance selection is affected by emotions and feelings from past experiences. For example, if spicy smells are your favorite scent, the reason could be that it makes you recall pleasant memories of an uncle or grandfather who smoked a spicy pipe tobacco.

Things That Affect Fragrances

Scents are affected by a person's age, skin color, health, and hormonal balance

•

Do not try fragrances on a day when you are under a lot of stress or are on a special kind of diet containing low or high fat. All of these things will affect the chemistry of your body and change the fragrance.

•

Extreme hot or cold temperatures will also affect the way a scent smells. Heat will cause a fragrance to give off a stronger scent. A scent that smelled great in February could be too overpowering by July or August.

•

Heat and sunlight also can change the scent of a perfume itself, so do not leave your perfume out on your dresser where the sun can affect it. Keep your fragrances capped tightly and store in a darkened drawer to keep the scent from changing.

•

When the days are hot, use talcum powder or dusting powder on your arms, neck, and shoulders to give you a feeling of luxury.

•

If you wear a fragrance for months and then all of a sudden it seems to change, don't blame the perfume. You can affect the scent by either starting or stopping a medication or perhaps changing your diet.

--------------- ❧ ---------------

If you become pregnant, your favorite perfume may smell differently on you.

Any hormonal change in the body or a severe illness or operation can cause a change in the way the perfume smells on your skin

•

No perfume smells exactly the same on two different women It is the body chemistry that determines the scent.

•

Since perfume is so expensive, do not buy the biggest bottle of a new fragrance the first time. Instead, try buying the cologne, which will not be as expensive. If it is a good fragrance, the essential scent will be exactly the same whether it is perfume or cologne. The only difference is the strength. If you keep the larger bottles of perfume and cologne for a long time, they tend to evaporate, leaving the scent stronger than you wanted.

General Tips

—— 🐟 ——

One good hint regarding perfume for the office is to wear a brisk, clean fragrance. And remember a little perfume can go a long way. You may not be able to smell it after awhile but it may prove to be a bit much for your fellow office workers.

•

Always buy good perfume. A cheap scent can really be a turn-off, especially in an office.

•

Remember it is best to have no fragrance at all than to have too much.

•

Perfumes are heavier than colognes so it may be best to wear the cologne at the office rather than the perfume.

•

Never use perfume or cologne to cover up a lack of bathing because your perspiration combined with your fragrance will give off a most unpleasant odor.

•

A clean fragrance or soft powder will give off a pleasant smell without being intrusive.

•

Crisp, soft scents are more easily associated with professionalism than heavier scents. This applies to after-shave lotions as well.

•

Do not apply perfume or cologne if you are going out into the sun to sunbathe because it may make your skin blotchy.

•

Put a small amount of your favorite fragrance in your bathwater. Add some bath oil or baby oil and it will help the fragrance last longer on your skin.

•

Apply fragrances to pulse points, such as behind your ears, your wrists, back of the knees, and ankles.

•

Be sure when you choose a fragrance that it matches your personality, not someone else's, and that it makes the statement that you want.

•

Try different fragrances on until you are comfortable with one and then wear it for awhile before purchasing. Walk around the store to let the fragrance adjust to your skin chemistry.

•

Know what type of perfumes to wear for different occasions. Don't wear an exotic scent first thing in the morning or a light floral cologne with an elegant evening gown. Wear the perfume that best fits the time of day and the occasion.

•

To use perfume correctly, do not mix the fragrances. If you can afford it, buy the soap, cologne, bath oil, powder, and perfume of your choice all in one fragrance.

•

A good perfume wardrobe should include a minimum of two fragrances: one for daytime and one for evening.

•

The outdoor smells are best for daytime and the more sophisticated romantic ones are best for the night. The woodsy and flower scents are very nice smells for the summer.

•

If you buy perfume and the scent stays too pungent, then it is probably not suitable for daytime wear. If you like the scent, purchase it in cologne which will not be as heavy.

•

The experts say that keeping cologne in the refrigerator does not prolong its life; however, it feels real refreshing to splash cool cologne on, especially if it is a hot day.

•

Do not apply perfume to your clothing or furs. It may stain.

•

Perfumes will not last as long on a woman who has dry skin so rub some natural oil or baby oil on your body to help make a perfume application last longer.

Perfume lotions will last longer on your skin. They are not only skin softening but carry a wonderful scent.

Some long-lasting forms of fragrances are cream, roll-on, compacts, and talcum.

•

Solid perfumes will not evaporate and will last longer.

•

When you use spray perfumes, hold the container only two inches away from your body so that the full impact of the mist is on your body and not in the air.

•

There is nothing wrong with having a perfume that is your signature to others, but do not get so narrow in your choice that you do not wear a variety of perfumes to suit different seasons and moods.

•

Decide what fragrances you like and dislike before you buy. You may like musk scents or floral scents, but generally speaking you will tend to lean toward a certain type and will be most happy wearing it.

•

Powders are great for tired feet.

•

When you buy perfume, check the seal to be sure that it has not been broken.

•

Perfume will evaporate if you do not cap it tightly or if you leave it exposed to the sun, sitting on your dressing room table. To prevent this problem, divide the perfume by using a small funnel to transfer some into a small, clean bottle for immediate use. Seal up the rest by melting paraffin drops of wax from a lighted candle around the stopper. Then store the bottle in its box in a cool, dark place.

•

Purse perfumes are a nice addition to your fragrance collection and usually have containers that are easily refillable. Also, most companies make a solid perfume in stick, compact, or roll-on form which is designed especially for the handbag and for travel. They are so nice to use to refresh yourself on a trip.

Making Your Home and Car
Smell Fragrant

Scented candles are great to use during the hot summer months to keep your home smelling refreshed. Candles create a mood of serenity and peace. I had a friend who once told me I needed to slow down and she bought me a candle and said, "You can't walk fast past a candle." I never forgot that and candles are now one of my favorite things. There are scented candles available in many of your favorite perfumes for you to use in your home. Or even a spray from a bottle will give your home an inviting atmosphere.

———— 🍂 ————

Spritz a small amount of your favorite fragrance on your pillow.

•

You can even shake a small amount of your fragrance into the car cushion.

•

Add some fragrance to your window curtains for a refreshing smell throughout the house.

•

You can add a soft subtle perfume to your drawers by using sachets or adding tiny drops of your favorite perfume.

•

Potpourri is a great way to add some romance and elegance to your home especially on special holidays like Christmas. Also, there are wonderful ones now available for year-round use.

*Mint gives a wonderful odor
and if you put a bunch in water
in a pretty jar, the odor will
sift throughout the room.*

Get some fragrant pomander balls for hanging in your kitchen to mask all sorts of unpleasant odors. You can use a lemon, lime, or the traditional orange as a base and then insert whole cloves to completely cover it, making sure that the cloves are very close together. Add some pretty ribbon for hanging. The ball will shrink with time but the scent will still remain.

•

Try creating an herbal scent by planting basil, mints, thyme, or rosemary plants in a recycled egg carton and putting them on a windowsill.

•

Put a drop of your favorite perfume on a cold light bulb. When you turn the light on, the fragrance will slowly spread throughout the entire room.

•

At Christmastime, or anytime for that matter, a nice fragrance is the mixture of cedar chips and pine needles.

•

Take all your specially scented guest soaps and put them in your lingerie drawer or place them in a pretty dish or basket and display them in a guest bath.

•

Use the sample fragrance cards that come from department stores and in magazines to give you a special fragrance by placing them in your drawers or between your sheets or towels.

•

If you leave books out for show, spritz a scent on a bookmark and let it hold your place in your book, as well as give a fresh smell to the room.

•

Sprinkle some fragrant bath powder between your sheets.

•

If you would like the woodsy and floral scents to permeate your home, spray the fragrance on your air conditioner to cool the air and refresh it at the same time.

There must be something to this fragrance phenomenon because it is a multimillion-dollar business. The right scent can add to a person's pleasure or it can also send them scurrying to find refuge from the unpleasantness of their surroundings whether it be a person or an environment. Learn to add pleasure. Your scent is one way that people remember you so choose your scent carefully.

Don't Look Now But Your Teeth, Hands, and Feet Are Showing

In your name I will lift up my hands
—Psalm 63:4

Teeth

A lovely smile is one of your most important beauty assets but many people do not smile because they are ashamed of their teeth. Natural tooth colors range from white to ivory and some have definite yellowish and even gray casts. When a person smiles, their beauty quotient goes up 50 percent. A smile projects warmth, understanding, or love and illuminates the face like no makeup can. It has been said the most important form of nonverbal communication is the facial expression and the most important body language on the face is the smile. If you think about the people you know with and without smiles, the ones who have a smile are more attractive and make you feel better because of their response to you. Why not smile at someone for no reason and make their day!

———— 🐚 ————

Do not use harsh products on your teeth such as some whiteners which will be damaging to your tooth enamel. Some toothpastes that have special tooth whiteners have proven to be too harsh on the enamel also.

•

For a cheaper way to whiten your teeth, brush once a week with baking soda in addition to your regular brushing.

•

Use toothpastes with fluoride and tartar control.

•

To prevent the buildup of plaque use dental floss. Your tooth-brush cannot remove all the food particles from between the teeth and close to the gums. Flossing prevents gum disease more effectively than any other form of home dental care.

•

Do not forget to brush your tongue while you are brushing your teeth.

---

*Do not use your teeth
to bite off thread, chew on pencils,
crack open nuts, or bite bones,
hard candy, or small pieces of ice.
This can cause little notches
in the front teeth.*

Your teeth are responsible for the contour of your face, making it look young or old. Many adults are now having their teeth straightened. See your orthodontist and you will never have to cover up your smile again.

•

If you have braces on your teeth, draw attention away from your mouth to your eyes with pretty makeup and an attractive hairstyle, and stay away from bright shades of lipstick. A soft pink or coral lipstick would be best. Do not be self-conscious about your braces because you will be admired for your deter-mination to improve your appearance.

•

Some of the ways to discolor your teeth are by drinking great amounts of tea and coffee without rinsing your mouth or brushing afterward Cigarette smoking is another cause of discoloration. Be sure that you brush and have your teeth cleaned frequently.

*

Achieving and maintaining a dental hygiene program should require almost as much time and attention as your makeup application does.

*

One of the many enemies of your teeth is sugar. It joins with the bacteria in your mouth to form acid and plaque that will eat your teeth and gums away. Be sure to clean your teeth as soon as possible after eating sugar and eat a lot of crunchy fibrous raw fruits and vegetables which will help clean the teeth.

*

Do not just see your dentist when you have a toothache. Regular checkups are extremely important and your teeth should be cleaned twice a year.

Hand Care

Your hands are seen just about as much as your face and good hand care contributes to the total look of grooming that completes the finished touch that says you care about yourself.

Talking with your hands is fine but an overabundance of movement can be distracting. Nevertheless, the experts say that talking with your hands is a positive sign. Graceful hand movements add to the look of a poised individual.

———— ❧ ————

Hands are a real age giveaway so use a lot of moisturizer and sunscreen.

*

Use a hand cream frequently when it is cold and keep an extra container in your desk at work and another in your handbag or car.

*

Every once in awhile it is good to coat your hands with a good moisturizer and sleep wearing white gloves to keep the moisturizer in. Try using baby oil or petroleum jelly.

*

You cannot get your hands, skin, or hair in proper condition in ten minutes or even ten days. It takes working at it all the time and it takes planning.

●

If your hands get stiff and tired during the day, give them some exercise. Stretch your fingers out as far as you can reach, then make a tight fist with each hand and repeat this procedure several times. Next, shake your hands from the wrists and pretend you are playing the piano in the air. This will make your hands feel more relaxed.

●

Remove super glue from your hands by soaking the glue with nail polish remover.

General Nail Care

Strong, beautiful nails make a big fashion statement and the artificial nail business is booming because so many women cannot grow their own.

Nails are made of protein and they grow from the skin rather than muscle or bone. It takes about six months for a nail to grow from bottom to top and as we get older that growth gets slower.

There are many theories for nail health. One, which does not seem to help as much as they first thought, is that Knox gelatin whether eaten or applied improves nail health. There is increasing evidence, however, that the addition of zinc to the diet might help your nails.

There may be a link between strong teeth and strong nails. However, a beauty plan that benefits your entire body will work for teeth and nails alike.

——— ॐ ———

Check your diet to see that it contains enough vitamin A and, of course, adequate protein.

●

Do not mistreat your nails. Even the hardest and most well-cared-for nails will break if they are used as tools, such as in prying off lids. Use a pencil to dial the telephone rather than your finger. Dialing a telephone, typing, filing, housework, and opening soda pop cans are some of the worst enemies for your nails. Begin to be aware of how you are abusing your nails and take some measures to stop that abuse.

•

Before beginning a garden project, dig your nails into a bar of soap and after your project they will clean up much better and faster. Better yet, wear a pair of gardening gloves.

If you have a nail biting habit,
you will be less likely to continue
if you keep your nails nicely manicured.
If you wear artificial nails, it is virtually
impossible to continue the habit.

If your nails get stained or have discolored tips, clean them by rubbing them for two or three minutes with a cotton swab soaked in lemon juice. Then, rinse the solution off, dry the nails, and buff.

•

Right-handed people have a faster nail growth on their right hands. People who type and stimulate the finger tips have nails that grow faster. Whether they stay long or not is determined by their care.

•

A lack of the mineral zinc can show up as white spots on the nails. Try adding brewer's yeast to your diet or add seafood on a weekly basis. The spots will not disappear but they will grow out with the nails as you make them more healthy. You may get spots on your fingernails just because of the wear and tear they endure or even from vigorous manicuring. You rarely see these spots on toenails that are better protected.

Dry, Peeling Nails

Brittle, damaged nails that are unkempt make negative image.

——— ❧ ———

The excessive and repeated use of polishes, nail hardeners, and removers will dry your nails. Most polish removers contain acetone which is a powerful solvent and is very drying to the nails. There are, however, some polish removers on the market that do not contain acetone and will say acetone-free on the label.

•

Dry, brittle nails are more commonly caused by abuse than by any specific deficiency in the diet.

•

Some things that dry out the nails and weaken them are detergents, glues, paint strippers, and other cleaning chemicals.

•

Spending a lot of time in the water will take its toll on improperly protected nails. Water leeches out your natural nail moisture and makes your nails brittle. Just as water lifts off dirt, it also lifts off the top layers of your nails and it causes polish to lose its sheen.

•

There are some good nail hardeners on the market that may help splitting nails.

•

Flaking and peeling nails are generally symptoms of excessive strain on the nail or an excessive amount of dryness. Purchase a good product that will put oil back into your nail and you will find that you can grow your nails longer with less breakage. Some wonderful products that are available now will add oil to your nails to keep them from peeling, cracking, and breaking. A good product that you might consider is a nail oil called DeLore which is a natural nail oil. Redken also puts out a good nail and cuticle oil. There are many others also, so consult a nail care specialist at your beauty salon.

•

Wear rubber gloves when you do dishes or whenever you have your hands in cleaning solutions.

•

Always use a good hand cream.

•

Rubbing a special cuticle cream into your cuticles and nails can help prevent cracking around the cuticle.

Polish

———— 🐦 ————

Weathered and wrinkled hands will look softer and shorter nails will look longer if you use frosted polishes. Remember to use colors so you do not draw attention to your hands. If you have older-looking hands any bright nail polish will draw attention to them.

•

A tan looks nice with the light shades of nail polishes. These shades will create a contrast with your tan.

•

One factor that determines the lasting ability of your manicure is the freshness of your polish.

•

Do not apply nail polish directly to the nail but always use an undercoat first.

•

Nails look best a little shorter and always when they are manicured and polished subtly.

•

It is best to apply two to three thin coats of polish rather than one heavy coat.

•

Nail enamels will be smooth and ready to use if you store them in the refrigerator.

Manicure

Make a good manicure a once-a-week project and then help your manicure to last all week by simply applying a topcoat each day. This seals in the polish and protects the nails.

—— 🐛 ——

Keep all your manicure equipment in a box or kit so you can save time when you want to do your nails. Some general items to put in your kit are emery boards, cotton balls, polish remover, polish, cotton-tipped swabs, a bowl for water or oil, and a small towel.

•

Keep the tools that you use for filing your nails and buffing in good condition. Make sure that your scissors or nail clippers are not dull.

•

Filing your nail a little more square than the oval shape, which goes too far into the side of the nail, will minimize breakage and is still flattering even on short nails. The tips of the nails should be very smooth.

—————————— 🐛 ——————————

File your nails in one direction instead of seesaw filing because when you seesaw file you undo what you have already filed.

Use a diamond deb file or an emery board since metal files are hard on the nails. It is usually better to file the nail rather than clip the nail.

If you clip your nails, be sure you always follow the nail's natural curve. Do not clip or file the sides of your nails, as this will encourage chipping.

•

Soak your nails in warm water, push the cuticles back, and then clean under the fingernails. Treat your nails to a warm oil bath and massage the cuticle to stimulate circulation. Wash hands thoroughly after soaking in a warm oil bath.

•

For extra protection for polished nails that tend to chip off on the ends, polish the back of the nail tips. This reduces the exposed surface area of the nail and strengthens the nail tips.

•

Polish from the small pinky to the thumb.

•

If you want your nail polish to stay on longer, try putting a coat of clear polish on the top and the tip of your nails each night.

•

To stimulate the growth of your nail, try massaging your nails and tips as often as possible increasing the circulation to the fingers. Whenever it is convenient, massage your fingers and hands to keep them flexible. Use a good cuticle cream and massage well into the fingertips.

•

Dip newly painted nails into ice water to make the polish dry quickly and evenly.

———————

A good manicure is the final touch for the total groomed look and is probably one of the most neglected. Even if you do not like to wear polish, your nails and hands should still be well-groomed with proper filing, cleansing, buffing, and moisturizing.

Artificial Nails

There is more interest than ever in the artificial nail or nail tip. Nail tips are good because they allow your nail to breathe and they simply grow out with your natural nail.

The artificial nails today are much tougher and more sophisticated than ever before and the methods used are less likely to damage the nail underneath.

Be sure that you go to a trained and reputable manicurist The do-it-yourself sets are not as good and the nails are precast so they tend to look unnatural. Also the glue is often too weak to ensure adhesion. A good manicurist can apply and file the nails to look like your own.

Foot Care

The feet have two main functions. They support the body and they propel us in walking. What happens to your feet affects your whole body including both your posture and your disposition. Most of us neglect our feet when they are tucked away in boots and pumps during the winter. Then suddenly, during warm weather they are on display. With a little time and attention you can look your loveliest right down to your toes.

Feet change and continue to change so a shoe that fits you fine at one time may not feel as good anymore. Feet can elongate or spread, particularly if you are on your feet a lot or you are overweight.

In the summer when we wear so many open-toed shoes and sandals it is imperative for you to have a good pedicure.

General Tips

——— 🐾 ———

To make feet look smaller, use a subtle shade of polish like a smoky rose.

•

Women with bony feet or heavily veined feet should always polish with soft colors.

•

Slenderize chubby toes with frosted shades.

•

Put an all-purpose talcum on your feet to help absorb moisture

•

When wearing socks with tennis shoes, be sure that they are all cotton

•

To freshen overworked feet soak them in ice water. This reduces any swelling

•

When purchasing shoes, buy them at the end of the day when your feet are the most swollen. This is one way to make sure that the shoes will not pinch later on.

•

Use fashion footwear to make the most of your feet. For example, if you have long narrow feet with slim ankles, choose a pair of sandals with ankle straps to give your feet a real fashion touch.

•

If you have thick ankles, then wearing simple thong sandals will look best.

Buy shoes with various heel heights to put pressure on different parts of the foot and leg.

If you have your feet beautifully manicured and you have pretty ankles, show them off with a delicate ankle bracelet.

•

When you massage your feet, include your legs and use a cream or lotion to stimulate circulation. Be sure that all the lotion residue is wiped off your toenails before you polish.

•

Spray your favorite scent on your feet.

•

Remember to use subtle shades if you want to make big feet look smaller. Use bold shades of polish if you want to show off your toes.

•

To keep your feet their healthiest, wear clean hosiery each day. Add a touch of talcum powder to the inside of your shoes each morning to keep both shoes and feet fresh.

•

Give your shoes time to air out by rotating the pair you wear each day.

•

For tired feet, soak them in lukewarm water with one cup of cider vinegar.

•

For warm weather, soft leather and fabric shoes are the best.

•

Puffiness in the feet and ankles is often caused by pressure on the veins at the back of the knee and is a complaint often heard from secretaries who sit with crossed legs for long periods of time. Try changing your position at work and if possible get your feet up in the air for a few minutes. Also, it is best not to cross your legs at any time because of the pressure it puts on the back of your leg causing varicose veins and incorrect posture.

•

There is a beauty aid now available to cover spider veins on your legs. It is a water-proof leg makeup that comes in a tube.

•

Consult your doctor if your varicose veins are large and unsightly.

Pedicure

Begin by giving your feet a good soaking in warm suds. After soaking your feet do not forget to push back the cuticles and clean under the toenails. Your tired feet will feel so good if you take time to soak them, so sit on the edge of the tub with your feet under the faucet and turn the water on full blast. Start with warm water and gradually increase it to a little hotter. Then after a few minutes, cool the water down again and dry your feet with a cotton towel. A good massage and rubdown of the feet will do wonders.

•

Scrub thoroughly with a soft brush.

•

Cut the toenails straight across instead of rounding them off.

•

Smooth the edges of the nails with an emery board using the coarse side of the board. The fine side is for finishing.

•

Remove the rough skin from your heels with a lotion formulated to remove calloused areas or try using a wet pumice stone, buffing lightly. To keep your heels and feet soft and smooth, rub on moisturizing cream at night. Use one that contains lanolin and this will help you to not get cracks on your heels.

•

Another tip for very dry skin on the feet is to apply a generous amount of petroleum jelly or baby oil before bedtime and then cover them with cotton socks. In the morning your feet will be silky soft.

•

Put cotton between your toes and then polish your toenails with two thin coats of polish.

•

Cornstarch makes a terrific foot powder.

•

Make sure that your feet are free of moisture before putting on stockings and shoes and then sprinkle a little talcum powder between the toes and on the soles of your feet.

A Well-Ordered Life

CHAPTER

12

Home Organization

And delight to see how orderly you are and how
firm your faith in Christ is.
—Colossians 2:5

Life takes organization. Getting organized will save you time and money, and will help eliminate unnecessary stress. When we have less stress and more time, we lead a more peaceful life with a calmer spirit. This allows our inner beauty to come through to others as we touch their lives.

We serve a God who is organized. This is evident by looking at the magnificent organization in the universe. Organization in a person's life brings serenity and allows the inner beauty that comes with a peaceful mind to shine through.

Organization does not have to be a burden or seem out of reach to someone who just feels they can't do everything they must do. Perhaps you need to eliminate some duties that are not necessary, and setting some priorities can certainly bring some perspective to your life. If you want to be able to do more than you think you can, then plan ahead and finish things ahead of the deadline. The fun in accomplishing tasks diminishes when you are always under pressure and stress. Some people seem to work better under those conditions but most people would welcome less stress and pressure.

You will find that being a list maker is very useful. Put your duties for the day in order of priority and mark them off as they are completed. Do not become a slave to the list. However, oftentimes there are too many people and too many things vying for our time during the day to be able to remember them all. When feeling overwhelmed, we just need to remember that tomorrow is another day.

A helpful way to keep track of your schedule is to purchase an organizer or notebook appropriate for your lifestyle and then use it every day.

Notebook Tips

Use a notebook that you can take with you when you go out so that you will have your information handy and will not have to guess at purchases. If you will keep a notebook that contains your color key, your life goals, books you want to read, and things to get done, then it will make your life easier for you to remember and you will do less backtracking. Many things we intend to get done, whether we work outside the home or are a homemaker, we do not get done because we simply forget to do them. This problem can be eliminated when things are written down.

——— 🙿 ———

Your small notebook organizer should include daily, weekly, and monthly appointments; an address section; a telephone number section; and a household planning section. One of your sections should contain your calendar where you can get a quick view of what you need to do daily as well as for the month. It can be as simple a duty as getting a report written or sending a birthday card.

•

Title one of your sections "Miscellaneous." Here you can keep information such as various phone numbers including those for emergencies, your husband's Social Security number, your car license numbers, clothes sizes of people you buy gifts for, or any other information that makes your life easier and helps you complete your tasks.

•

The secret is to use the notebook and to not leave it sitting in the drawer. Keeping a calendar of appointments and things to do will keep you from overlapping responsibilities and will help you to remember important dates.

•

Another thing that might be valuable to you is a separate little book with blank pages. Here you can write down things that you want to remember either from what someone has said or from a special program on the radio. If it touches your heart, then write it down so that you will not forget what was said. You might also want to write down your thoughts and feelings for that day. This is your memory book and you will refer to it year after year.

Calendar Tips

—— ❧ ——

Get a big wall calendar and use a different color pen for every member of the family. They can each mark their own obligations, meetings, and other appointments. Then everyone can see what each member of the family is doing and when.

•

A yearly calendar gives an overall view of the year, a monthly calendar can be glanced at for appointments that are not on the standard routine, and a daily calendar gives you a perspective for the day.

•

Hang the calendar in an accessible area that makes it easy to see and use. If it is accessible, all members of the family will be more likely to write their appointments and activities on it. It is another way to communicate and keep everyone informed.

Family Organization

When you begin to organize, begin with yourself and your family first and then move into other areas of your life such as your job and your home. Being part of a family and keeping it running smoothly without too much pressure on one member takes planning and cooperation. Be fair because resentment does not make for a happy atmosphere Every person in a family has a different personality and will have different priorities for their own way of organizing their lives, but everyone in the family also has an obligation to help make the family surroundings pleasant. Remember habits are established when children are young and will carry over into their adult lives. It is easier to learn how to do things orderly as a child than changing set ways as an adult. A good example is taking a few minutes in the morning to make the bed. If you have not been taught or have not developed good organizational habits, it is not too late to change some bad habits into good ones. Sometimes the motivation to change comes from simply an awareness of how we clutter our lives.

—— ❧ ——

If you have promised to do something with your family for the night and another intrusion vies for your time, give first priority to your family.

•

Lavish praise for jobs well done.

———————————— ❧ ————————————

Everyone needs a certain amount of space for their personal things, so create a special place for each member of the family.

————————————————————

When children are small, create good habits by making a chart and giving smile faces or stars for a job well done.

•

Keep a sponge by the sink in the bathroom so that each member of the family can wipe up the sink and cabinet after themselves.

•

Use paper cups for drinks instead of glasses during the day and it will save dishes.

•

If you have a large family, each child should have a different color basket for their dirty clothes. Then their colors can be washed and put in the basket for them to put away

•

Have a drawer specifically for first-aid items

•

Each member of the family should get in the habit of clearing their dishes from the table and taking them to the sink. Then whoever has dish duty will have an easier job.

•

Create specific places for specific things like the hair dryer or curling iron. There are some wonderful hangers you can make or buy for hanging them on the wall.

•

Put things away after each use. Simple but often not done.

•

Do some things the night before, such as picking out clothes, or making lunches, to take stress out of the morning school rush.

•

Don't waste time looking for frequently used items. Instead, keep all those items such as scissors, tape, pencils, and note-paper together in one place in the kitchen, bedroom, or other often-used rooms. This will eliminate the problem of having to search for something when you need it.

•

When cleaning your garage, eliminate all unnecessary things and group all like items together such as paints, garden tools, etc.

Kitchen Organization

The kitchen is a good family gathering place and therefore needs special organizational attention. Whether you are looking for spices or pans, being able to find things when cooking is a stress buster. The kitchen is also one of those places that can get the messiest in the shortest time. One meal or even a small snack can leave a mess and clutter that will hinder the next meal and make it harder to prepare. Returning items to their proper place will help keep this room pleasant and easier to utilize again.

———— 🐌 ————

When you start to organize your cupboards, begin with the one closest to the sink and methodically go around the kitchen.

•

Take everything out of your cupboards. Clean, and throw out or give away anything that is no longer used. Make room so that items such as your bowls are not falling on your head when you open the door.

•

Store all seldom-used items in a kitchen overflow box.

•

When you put things back, put the most often-used items in the front and the seldom-used ones in the back or on the highest shelves.

Odd items such as vases and odd dishes should be boxed and stored to reduce kitchen clutter.

Eliminate clutter in your utensil drawer by putting frequently used items such as wooden spoons, ladles, whisks, spatulas, and rubber scrapers into a crock or ceramic pot that can sit on your counter.

•

Keep all of your knives sharpened so that they are ready to use.

•

Use a plastic divider in the junk drawer to organize tacks, nails, batteries, glue, etc.

•

Keep your pantry just for food—no papers items, books, or toys. Label shelves according to foods such as soups, fruits, vegetables, and cereals. Keep the baking section separate with flour, sugar, baking soda, and mixes. Keep the packaged items such as dressing mixes in a large jar or a small box to keep from getting scattered.

•

Keep all items such as tea bags, flour, crackers, noodles, and coffee in jars.

•

Store on the same shelf appliances that work together such as mixing bowls, mixers, and measuring cups.

•

Keep all pans together and if you have enough room line the shelf with paper, and draw an outline of the pan, and then store it in its designated place.

•

Use lazy Susans in the refrigerator to hold items such as sour cream, cottage cheese, jellies, and mustard. Then you can just spin to get the item you want.

Keeping Surroundings Less Cluttered.

People who get what they want out of life learn to eliminate clutter in order to concentrate on what is important. Clutter, whether in the kitchen, bedroom, or bathroom, can create a feeling of a lack of control. Looking through clutter to find simple things yields frustrations and ends in stress.

——— ❧ ———

Pick up as you go. Do not let everything go and then pick up at one time all that you have left for days. Keep your world pleasant and uncluttered.

•

Make your bathroom an easy place to clean by keeping on hand a small plastic wastebasket with all the brushes, sponges, and cleaners needed to clean the room.

•

Our surroundings can sap our energy. Be sure you have a comfortable bed and uncluttered bedroom.

•

Eliminate cluttered areas in your kitchen. If you do, getting dinner on the table or doing baking will not take as much energy or cause as much irritation.

•

Organize your handbag so that the small irritation of having to search for something is removed and efficiency is increased.

Planning Ahead

Doing things ahead of time is one of the best tips for organization and time management. Think ahead. If your summer shoes need repairing, then get them done ahead of time so that they will be ready when you need them. If your bike needs fixing before spring, do it before you need it. Get your lawn mower repaired in the winter so you do not have to wait to use it in the summer. Never go through life without a plan.

———— 🍂 ————

Buying more than one item of something saves a lot of time. Do this with groceries as well as items such as underwear, stockings, and handkerchiefs.

•

Keep things on hand for emergency forgotten special days and it will add to your efficiency. An example would be birthday candles.

•

Buy some items that would be good gifts for weddings, showers, and birthdays when they are on sale. Then you will always have something on hand for an emergency or when you do not have time to shop. This works especially well when you run into a good sale.

•

Keep a supply of wrapping paper, string, Scotch tape, and boxes handy to wrap gifts. It will make your iife easier when you need these supplies.

•

When you are cooking, fix extra portions and freeze them. This works well for dishes like lasagna. Then on that hurried evening you can just pop it in the oven and put your feet up for a while.

•

Plan your laundry time so that you will be able to take the clothes out and fold them when the dryer is finished. This will save fluffing up the clothes or even ironing.

---

*Start eliminating unnecessary tasks.
Many times we do them simply
because we have always done them.*

Include the people in your world in the things that you do by delegating duties. Besides taking pressure off of you this will make the person you ask feel good about being needed and useful.

•

Americans do not read as much as they should. Always keep a book in your handbag or car so that if you have to wait in your car or office you can catch up on your reading.

•

It is important to plan your days and then stick to the plan. Making a list will help you.

•

If you are not getting things done as you would like, take a good look at your schedule and see if you are trying to do too much. If you are, set some priorities.

•

You should always be able to revise your plans. Do not pursue a plan to the bitter end if you can see that some revision needs to be done.

13

Time Management

*There is a time for everything, and a season for
every activity under heaven.*
—Ecclesiastes 3:1

Time management means using your time wisely so you
can get everything done in the limited time that you have. It
has been shown that if you could save one hour each working
day during a normal career, you could add the equivalent of six
years to that career. It becomes a habit to save time, so begin to
break some bad habits and replace them with good ones until
finally they become second nature to you.

How do you become more effective in plugging up time-
waster holes? Begin identifying where your time goes during
one week by writing down how much time you spend doing
various tasks. Also keep track of breaks and interruptions.
This will probably cause you to make some interesting discoveries. You might find that you waste time the same way during
a specific time period each day. When you identify this, you
can plug the hole. You also might discover that there are
certain people who waste your time every day. The important
thing is that you begin to see precisely how and where your
time gets away from you.

You will be more productive at various times of the day. Do
the most concentrated and hardest tasks at these times.

A big time waster is not only doing the wrong things, but
doing things the wrong way. Manage your time. Do not let the
time manage you.

Time management is important but so is relaxation and if
you will learn to be better organized you will have more time

for relaxation and recreation. I hope some of these tips will help you to realize your dreams. You can do it if you want to.

Time Wasters

Do not waste time in the things you do or in harboring anger and bitterness.

•

Work by appointment. If you have a busy schedule, then make a list of things that need to be done by a certain time and give yourself time limits. You will be surprised how much you can accomplish.

Divide large tasks into several small ones and they will not seem so overwhelming.

Worrying can immobilize people and be a real time waster. Most of the time, the things we worry about never come to pass. If you are worrying about something you have no control over, ask God to take the burden and take care of it and then you need to leave it there.

•

If you start a task with the correct attitude, it will not seem as arduous and it will get finished faster

•

If you have a list of things that need to be done, start with the one that you dislike the most and then progress to the more pleasant ones as you become more tired.

•

Take short breaks and some deep breaths to refresh yourself.

•

Plan something special for yourself when you have finished a particular task you have been dreading and avoiding. Then when it is done you have two things to be happy about: the task you have completed and the reward you will receive.

•

Eliminate frustration by realizing that it is impossible to do everything you would like to do absolutely perfectly all the time, all by yourself, exactly when you planned to do it.

•

Don't flip the TV on and then spend the whole evening watching shows you never intended to watch and actually did not even enjoy. This is a real time waster so get control of your time and use it wisely. Make sure that you are following your schedule and not someone else's.

•

When you schedule your time, think of it in the same way that you budget your money. Invest some in the future and enjoy the present. It is the unscheduled people that never have enough time to get everything done and relax.

Procrastination

——— 🐝 ———

Do not put off until later what you should be doing now. Procrastination is a big time waster and sometimes when we put a project off, it may require more time later. If you admit that you are procrastinating you will be halfway to being able to stop wasting time and start forming some better habits.

•

Just jump in and get tasks done. It is amazing what a boost this can be to your day and you will find that a great burden is lifted when a task you really did not want to do is finished.

•

If you put off what you need to do, then worrying about what you have to do robs you of energy and pretty soon you are too tired to do the task.

•

If you wait for perfect conditions to do things then you will never get anything done because there seldom are perfect conditions.

•

Do not start a big job late in the day when you are tired or when you will not be able to finish it. Sometimes you just have to say that tomorrow is another day.

Telephone Time Savers

——— 〜 ———

One time waster and energy expender can be the time you spend on the telephone. Block most of your calls for one period of the day and it will help with telephone efficiency. An answering machine will help you accomplish this.

•

Reorganize the junk drawer or accomplish some other task while talking on the telephone.

•

Keep telephone numbers that you call frequently easily accessible.

•

If your life requires a good deal of telephone time, install a long cord or a portable telephone so you can move about freely doing other things.

•

Keep most of your conversations centered on the reason for calling.

General Time Management Tips

Disorganized people seem to work harder than organized people because they do not manage their time efficiently. They work extra hours to get everything done and they end up tense. Disorganized people tend to become slaves to the clock. They work to beat the clock rather than making time work for them. The more that you are organized the less anxiety you will feel.

If you go to a seminar on time management or read a book on how to do something and then do not put it into practice, it is like not knowing it at all. To just hear or read something without acting on it is in itself a waste of time.

——— ❧ ———

Always have something handy to do so that you don't waste any time while waiting for an appointment or some other delay.

•

Be prepared. A lot of energy is expended just gathering tools to do a task. Sometimes it takes twice as long to gather up things as to do the job itself.

•

Relaxation is not wasted time. All of us need some time for ourselves so plan it into your schedule.

——————————— ❧ ———————————

Combine activities like doing your exercises while watching television or using the exercise bike while catching up on your reading.

If you have a lot of errands to do and no time to do them, save precious time by hiring a teenager to deliver some things to your home.

•

Always shop with a list when going to the grocery store so that you do not forget items and have to make return trips. Also, go at a time when there are fewer lines.

•

Sometimes we attempt to do something difficult, like our tax preparation, that would take a professional only minutes to do. Let professionals do some of the really time-consuming jobs.

If your schedule is continually interrupted, learn to reschedule your day. Leave enough time to do the things that you have planned to do so that those interruptions do not throw you off schedule.

•

Set up a good filing system for bills, receipts, recipes, etc. The purpose of a filing system should be to retrieve something not to store it.

•

Schedule those activities that require greater concentration during your peak production times. All of us have certain times during the day when we work more efficiently. Some people are morning people, some are evening.

———————————— ≥ ————————————

Fix the kids' lunches for the next day while you are fixing dinner. This saves time and cleanup.

———————————————————————

You can give yourself 10 or 15 minutes more sleep on weekday mornings by planning the week's wardrobe ahead of time during a half hour on Saturday. Write down and put together the clothes you plan to wear for the week including shoes, hosiery, and jewelry. Include in your plan after-work dates, important meetings, and more casual days.

•

If you find you cannot keep things neat no matter how hard you try, do not just assume that you are poorly organized. Maybe you have a flawed environment that can be changed to be more efficient and pleasant.

•

Keep a basket in the top of the entryway closet for mittens, hats, etc. Keep a basket for snowboots on the floor of the closet.

This will eliminate both entryway clutter and having mud tracked through the house.

•

Keep an umbrella in the car for emergencies.

•

Whether or not you bag your own groceries, make sure that all foods that are alike are packed together. When canned goods, frozen foods, or meats are packed together, they are easier to put away.

•

Always shop with a list and if possible buy in bulk. Save time by writing your list on an envelope and then putting the coupons inside.

•

Rounding out your bills to the nearest dollar will make balancing your checkbook easier.

•

Do more shopping by mail from reputable mail order catalogs.

•

Put your favorite recipe page numbers in the front of the cookbook so they are easy to find.

•

If you cannot find time to go to an aerobics class, then use workout videos to save time and keep on your schedule.

•

Keep things simple. Get rid of junk overload.

To sum up: Doing things ahead of time, planning ahead, and having an environment where things can be easily found are three of the best organizational tools you can have. This sounds easy and it is. Just get started organizing by looking at each area of your life and making changes one step at a time. Otherwise, if you thought you had to be completely organized by tomorrow, you would be overwhelmed. Above all, keep things in your life handy and uncluttered.

14

Goal Setting

*I press on toward the goal to win the prize for which
God has called me heavenward in Christ Jesus.*
—Philippians 3:14

All of us have things that we do not like to do. But sometimes getting organized enough in your life to get a fresh start or shaping up a plan for improving your image can take months or even years. However, if you do not set some goals those changes will never take place.

Head and heart goals are fine but if you really want to accomplish those goals, it will require planning and then recording those plans on paper. There is an interesting statistic from a study that was done to determine why some people reach their goals and why some do not. The study concluded that very few people ever reached their life goals. In fact, only 3 percent of the people reached their goals and the one common factor these people had was that the goals were written down so they could see them every day. Many of us wish we could achieve higher goals, but they are just that—wishes. Accomplishing your heart's desires takes planning and effort.

———— 🐛 ————

Decide what needs to be changed and set some goals on how to get started. Decide what cannot be changed and accept it. Go through your lists and circle the things that you could improve and put a check by the things that you need to learn to accept.

•

Identify your goal, whether it is extra weight you want to take off or finishing up your college degree. Target your goal and then work a plan to achieve your objectives.

•

Determination, self-control, and consistency are three things that are needed to reach goals.

•

Eliminate all your excuses such as being too busy, too old, or too tired for not reaching your goals. Now move beyond those excuses and take the first step.

Surround yourself with positive,
supportive people who believe in you
and improve your life.

Have your goals before you every day. Write them on a small card and put them in places in your house or at work where they can be read often. You need a clear picture of what you want to accomplish. Writing things down helps you to accomplish this.

•

Write your one-year goals first, then six-month goals and then three-month goals. You gain a much more positive outlook in accomplishing what you want this way because you realize that something you could never do for a month, you could do for a week.

•

Once you have identified some of your problem areas, you need to analyze in greater depth those things that you really want to improve and how much time and effort it will take.

•

Once you have gained an understanding of those areas that you want to improve, it's time to take action.

•

Get specific. For instance, if you want to lose weight, you need to come up with the exact number of pounds you need to lose to reach your goal and the time it will take you to accomplish that goal. If you want to improve your marriage, identify the areas that need changing. Begin to measure your progress by spending one evening a week alone with your spouse.

•

Get cheerleader people to help you over some of the humps. Enlist a good friend to help cheer you toward your goal.

•

Learn to communicate. Lack of communication causes so many people to lose sight of a goal and give up on themselves, their marriages, and sometimes just life. If you do not communicate, many unresolved things are harbored and they can end up as negative responses and actions keeping you from positively pushing on toward your goal.

•

Don't be easily discouraged. Realize that just because you have committed yourself to a goal does not mean you will never lose ground. It happens to all of us from time to time but do not let a small setback make you abandon your goal altogether.

•

Do not condemn yourself to failure. When you do, you are letting negative thinking reinforce your thoughts of failure.

•

Plan something special for yourself when you reach your goal.

•

Every time you are tempted to give up concentrate on the positive reward you will receive

•

If what you have set to accomplish will take more than a month, then set intermediate goals

•

Reward yourself for achieving progress toward your goals. The rewards do not have to be expensive. Something as simple as a rose set on your desk will lift your day. When you give yourself a reward you are saying that you believe in your ability to set a goal and achieve it.

Goals are the specific end results that you want and activities are those things that you do to meet those goals. A goal has to be specific and concrete. Sometimes a goal is simply realizing that what you need to do is to enjoy what you already have. You may think that you are in the same place that you were yesterday but what you need to realize is that you will never be there again, for you have moved into a fresh new day. It's what you do with it that really counts.

Learning to set life goals gives you an identity. Many midlife crises come when you fool around all of your life without setting specific goals and then you begin to realize that you do not have many more years on this earth to do what you want to do.

Jack LaLanne said something that I really liked. He said, "You have twenty-four hours every day to do what you want, and you are the sum total of how you use those hours." He certainly is the visible proof of someone who set a goal and accomplished it.

Everyone's goals are different and that is what makes you different. God makes no two flowers, snowflakes, or people exactly alike.

PART 4

Organizing for Beauty

CHAPTER
15

Start With the Closet

*Everything should be done in a fitting
and orderly way.*
—1 Corinthians 14:40

Very few women feel their closet is adequate. However, you need to understand your closet before you summon a wrecking crew and carpenters to whip up something expansive and organizable—a nice, big closet that you feel good about.

What do you need to understand about your existing closet? The two things you need to examine are 1) its organization (or lack thereof), and 2) its contents (including stuff that could be put elsewhere, such as the curb).

What's wrong with your closet? Are you unable to find anything? Then, investing in new clothes will not solve your problem.

But, you say, you need to improve your look dramatically? Buying new expensive suits and dresses is not the answer if you already have a problem finding things and putting them together each day. Also, you might discover some new looks right in your present closet if it were just organized. Sometimes, dressing smartly is not dependent on new clothes or how much space you have but instead how successful you are at using what you already have.

Messy closets are as big an energy waster as unorganized office files, so take a long, objective look at your closet. The truth is there is more space than you think.

You will need a closet organization system that will work for your lifestyle. But first you need to start with a clean closet. So consider these quick tips to help you get organization back into an important part of your life. Start feeling good about your closet.

Closet Weeding

—— &. ——

Take everything out. Do the same thing with your dresser drawers and anywhere else you keep clothes that you seldom see. This will give you a different perspective of your wardrobe. You can easily weed out unwearables or nonwearables and you will be left with a clearer picture of what goes together and what you need.

•

Take out-of-season clothes from the closet. Store them elsewhere. Since it is too hard to see what you have when everything is mixed together, hang evening clothes and out-of-season clothes in different places than the closet you use each day. Also, you can store out-of-season clothes in garment bags.

•

Remove all those clothes that fit you ten years ago. Usually, clothing this old is out-of-date. Even if you are lucky and reach your honeymoon weight again, you will want a new look.

•

Let go of those possessions from yesterday that are stuffed into closets, under beds, and in dresser drawers. Unclutter your life.

•

Some items need to be discarded not because they are old but because you know it was a mistake to buy them. Opening your closet each morning and facing old mistakes is not good. It is certainly not a way to make dressing a pleasant activity.

•

You might think about moving little-used clothing to the back of your closet. If you have not worn it for a long period of time, get rid of it.

•

If your weight varies, remove the clothes that do not fit and make room for new clothes.

•

Unless you dearly love them, don't hang onto clothes hoping for a weight goal to be reached. Chances are, you will want some new clothes when you reach your goal. Keep in your closet only those clothes you really wear.

Be sure you have followed these closet cleaning rules before you shop. Everything that is too small, the wrong color, or the wrong line or style should be removed. Put aside those clothes that need mending. Give to charity those clothes that no longer work for you. Your closet may look bare but it is impossible to see what you need or add to your coordinates if your closet is jammed full of unwearables.

If you have done your closet weeding properly, everything that remains in your wardrobe should be something you are currently wearing or is at least wearable. Everything in your closet should hang without wrinkles and should be easy to remove without tugging. Don't let items get out of sight and lose some good wearing times.

The big stress remover in closet organization is to keep everything in view so you do not have to uncover boxes to find something you want.

Maximizing Closet Space

To get your closet to better serve you, put all of your blouses, skirts, sweaters, pants, shirts, and jackets together. Try all the possible combinations that will work together. Then coordinate them with accessories.

•

Divide your clothes into sections: dresses, casual or sporty blouses, and dressy blouses. This makes it easy to pull an outfit together.

•

Keep all your classic styles. They are wearable year after year. For example, a jacket with a length that is not too long or too short or a lapel that is not too narrow or too wide is considered classic. Keep it. Accessories can update these clothes and make them look fresh and new.

•

Use multiple clip-on hangers for skirts and blouses to conserve space.

•

Use modular shelves and basket storage systems to get maximum use of space. There are many types available at your local discount store.

Put things back where they belong. Ask yourself, "How will I find it next time if I don't put it back where it belongs?"

Use multilevel rods to maximize closet space. Hanging jackets on top and slacks on the lower level will make some areas of your closet do double duty.

•

Invest in sturdy, well-made hangers. They will help your clothes keep their shape longer. They usually go on sale along with plastic see-through shoe boxes.

•

Be sure your storage space is clear and dry. Damp basements may provide space, but they may also promote mildew damage.

•

Plastic or ceramic hooks are great for hanging robes, nightgowns, and bulky items. They can be installed on the back of closet doors, bathroom doors, or other out-of-the-way places.

•

Place those clothes most often worn in the front part of your drawers. This will help keep the drawer from looking like a whirlwind went through it.

•

Keep articles you most often use in drawers that are easiest to pull out.

•

Hang a scented deodorizer in each closet and change the scent frequently.

———————

An organized closet simplifies getting dressed and leads to an organized and happy day. Get into the habit of keeping your closet in order so you can continue to add coordinated items. Resolve to clean your closet at the beginning of each new season.

Finding Your Accessories

——— ૨৯ ———

Keep jewelry, lingerie, and belts in specially designated places. For example, all necklaces should have their own place. There are many hanging racks available to keep them from becoming tangled. A board with pegs or hooks will keep those necklaces and chains in order. They can be put on the back of a closet door or hung against an out-of-the-way wall.

•

Belts should be put in plastic see-through boxes for easy identification. Watch for sales on this item. They can be a bit expensive but they normally go on sale about three times a year.

•

Mug racks and hanging extenders work well for hanging belts and jewelry.

•

A separate dresser tray for often-used jewelry or watches can be a big help. This is especially good for jewelry you wear every day.

•

To keep earrings separate and easy to find, use a mechanic's multiple-drawer workbench organizer that is normally used for screws or small parts. This doesn't sound too glamorous but it sure does the trick. It can be stored on a shelf in your closet.

•

Remove all your shoes from the pile on the floor of your closet. Clear plastic shoe boxes provide easy storage for your shoes and you can quickly find those shoes you want to wear. To save money, simply use the box each pair came in and mark the end boldly with the proper shoe description for easy identification. You can also use a narrow shelf or a hanging shoe bag to keep your shoes off the floor. This not only helps your closet organization but also your temper when you can't find that second shoe.

Accessories are very important to expand your wardrobe and they need special organization so you can utilize them easily. They can be easily forgotten if they cannot be easily found. Accessories are a good way to extend your budget because without a lot of investment they can add to your wardrobe and make it look different.

16

Let's Go Shopping

*She is energetic, a hard worker, and watches
for bargains.*
—Proverbs 31:17,18 TLB

When you have your closet in order you are then ready to add some intelligent buys to your wardrobe. The more knowledge you have, the better steward you can be when spending your hard-earned money. When people have little knowledge about what is best for them in line, proportion, or color they end up making bad purchases which generally sit in their closet.

So many people go to town to shop and have no idea what they want or what they need to add to their wardrobe. The result is a closetful of a mixture of clothes often bought on impulse. Unless there is some forethought given to what is already in your wardrobe and where you are heading with your coordinates, this can be very costly to the pocketbook. Many clothes, therefore, end up not ever being worn and making us wonder why in the world we bought them.

Since most of us need some guidelines when shopping to insure the most practical purchases, here are some good tips.

General Shopping Tips

Know your figure well before you shop. Do this by measuring your proportions and keeping in mind your problem areas such as where you are thick, heavy, long, or short. Do not let the clerk talk you into something that is not right for you. In order to accomplish this you have to know your own figure and know what is right and what is not right for you.

Designer clothes are often put together in such a way that the pieces are already coordinated. This makes shopping very easy and when you buy the additional pieces you build a wardrobe with easily interchangeable looks from day to evening.

If you are buying a suit and there are slacks to match, buy them. You will find that one day you will want to wear the trouser look and another day the suited look and it is very hard to match the color if it is not from the same selection or dye lot. There will be many times that you wish you would have completed the outfit.

Learn to recognize brand names and quality clothes before you buy. Better-quality clothing will hang better and wear longer.

Getting the Best Value for Your Money

—— ❧ ——

Know your best colors. See chapter 2 on color.

•

When shopping, wear comfortable clothes and be sure they are easy to slip on and off in the dressing room.

•

Bring stockings and heels if you do not want to wear them so you can see what the completed outfit will look like. It is hard to buy a dressy dress in knee socks.

•

Never go shopping when you are tired or in a hurry because this is when you will make your biggest buying mistakes. Shopping takes patience and persistence to find what is right for you.

•

Buying on impulse can cause some shopping errors.

•

If possible, shop early before the stores become crowded with people.

•

If you know about an upcoming sale and you see something you like, try the garment on ahead of time to get the proper size and style. Then on the sale day you can just purchase the outfit without having to try it on.

•

To get a good idea of your wardrobe needs, ask yourself some questions before you make your purchases: How do I appear to others? How do I wish to appear?

———————— 🐌 ————————

Get to know a favorite salesperson who can help you keep from making a purchase mistake.

Other questions to ask yourself before a purchase are, "Will it fit easily into my wardrobe?" "Does it fit my personality?" "Is it financially feasible?" "Will it work into my lifestyle?"

•

Do not buy something just because it has a low price. No matter how little you paid for something it is no bargain unless you wear it.

•

Take a clipping from the inside seam of an article of clothing that you are trying to match. Oftentimes you will find many shades of the color you are trying to match and this will help avoid a wrong choice.

•

To get the best fit, always try the garment on before purchasing and study both your front and back in the mirror. Sometimes we forget to check the look from the backside.

•

Steer clear of trendy colors, fabrics, and styles unless that is your personality or you have a large wardrobe budget. They will not stay in fashion very long and will date your style.

•

When shopping it is best to buy quality in shoes, handbags, coats, suits, and items that you will be wearing many times. You can spend less on accessories and items such as lingerie, hosiery, and perhaps some bargain blouses and sweaters.

•

If the store will let you take clothing home on approval, do it. This is a good way for you to see how it fits with your existing wardrobe before you buy it. A good purchase is one that you can move through at least four to six items that you already have in your wardrobe. For example, a sweater or blouse should coordinate with various slacks, skirts, suits, etc. Color plays an important part in coordinating your wardrobe.

•

If you want to save money on clothing then remember that the versatility of the garment is more important than quantity. Each piece that you purchase should be extremely flexible and create different looks when it is worn with other accessories and separates.

•

When you shop, have in mind what you are looking for in line, style, and color so that you do not make poor purchases. This will help you extend your wardrobe rather than just add to it.

•

The springtime is a good time of year to consider a suit or coat purchase.

•

It is important to know the difference between a garment that is too small or tight and a garment that is supposed to be snug and hug your shoulders. Also know the difference between oversized, as in perfectly loose, and just plain enormous.

•

It is important to buy the best that you can afford. For example, two elegant cashmere sweaters in the correct colors for your wardrobe will last many seasons and will always make you feel elegantly dressed.

Making Intelligent Decisions

—— ❧ ——

Always check the construction of the garment, such as the seams, buttons, button holes, width of the hem, and sewing construction. Keep in mind that the quality of a garment is more obvious in a solid-colored garment.

•

A well-sewn seam sometimes has two lines of stitching. If the item you are planning to buy is torn along the seam, it has either not been well made or has not been inspected.

•

Check the zipper to see that it lies flat and even. If the zipper is puckered or curling, then chances are the entire garment was not well made and will never hang right.

•

The hems of a skirt or dress should hang evenly and the stitching should be secure. Quality clothing generally has adequate hems and seams.

•

Be sure to check that the lining in your garment fits well and does not pull the outer fabric.

•

Be sure your fabric pattern, whether stripe or plaid, matches. It should match along the seam lines and pockets.

•

Another tip is to consider the fit. Too many women buy clothes for style or color without bothering to take into consideration the way the clothing is cut or how it fits. Unless something fits well, it will not do much for you regardless of its design or its cost.

•

Learn to anticipate your needs ahead of time and shop for these more expensive items during close-out season sales.

•

If you will buy well-made and versatile clothing you will not need as many clothes.

•

Purchases should be classic enough to go from season to season. This also applies to your shoes. When you find a shoe that lasts and is a shape that works for you, then buy several different colors.

Choose a dress or garment that directs the eye to your best feature.

Know whether something is worth altering. There is a difference between a garment that is too small and a garment that is out of proportion and will need only a little altering to make it wearable. However, do not buy something that has to be altered too much because you may lose the shape.

•

Take time to analyze your past mistakes in purchasing. Look at your real fashion bloopers and ask yourself why you bought them. Fashion bloopers occur when you are talked into a purchase by a pushy clerk, when you have neither the time nor patience to find what you really want, or when it is a "bargain" that you cannot pass up.

•

Watch for sales and shop for warm-weather clothes in January and cold-weather clothes in July to save money. Shop March or April for summer clothes that are still new for the season but before they are picked over.

More Good Shopping Tips

What is in your closet and not what is in the stores should dictate your purchases.

•

Variety in colors and patterns should be introduced into the wardrobe by purchasing less expensive pieces.

•

Shop with your makeup on and your hair styled. You will be better able to tell what a garment will look like if you look presentable.

•

Shop for fabric that goes with other items in your wardrobe. A good polyester or wool blend and a good gabardine are all quality fabrics. Buy fabrics that look and feel expensive.

•

Polyester knits are not versatile pieces to coordinate with your wardrobe and they do not give a fashionable look.

•

Buy tweeds and soft plaids to extend the solids in your wardrobe.

•

Buy silk blouses and dresses to add elegance to your wardrobe. They now have available many wonderful washable silks for those who have small children.

•

Keep to a budget and you will feel better about your purchases.

•

Take someone with you that you trust to confirm your opinion on your purchase. Choose someone who will be honest with you about the line and style best for you.

•

Always stand in front of a full-length mirror to get an overall picture of the garment on you.

•

Know your style when shopping and resolve to never again buy anything that doesn't give you that special feeling when you wear it. These special feeling clothes are the ones in your closet that you will wear.

•

To train your eye to be more aware of lines and proportion, study store windows, fashion magazines, and people on the street and try to figure out why a particular outfit looks balanced or unbalanced.

•

Learn to pick your clothes for comfort as well as style because confident and powerful people need to look at ease in their clothes.

•

Being comfortable in clothes does not necessarily mean looking sloppy.

•

To keep nylon fabrics from yellowing, add some baking soda to both the wash and the rinse water.

•

To keep colors in a newly purchased article of clothing from running, rinse with vinegar in the water to set the color.

————

Sometimes new trends such as a new skirt length are hard to accept. Often it takes time before your eyes have a chance to adjust and that fashion becomes comfortable for you. Think of it this way—the changing fashions add identity to each era that passes.

Looking your best doesn't just happen. It takes time and motivation. You need to enjoy what you wear. That is the whole point of dressing and feeling good about yourself.

Investment Shopping

With the dollar not able to buy as much as it used to, it is even more important to know how to investment shop.

Investment dressing involves weighing the number of times an item can be worn versus the cost. For example a raincoat may be a good purchase where it rains a lot and probably not a good investment if only worn two or three times a year in a sunny climate. If you buy clothing keeping in mind how many times you will be able to wear it, you will get more for your dollar. That is really what investment dressing is all about. It is being able to wear things in many different ways for many different occasions. For instance, if you purchase a quality gabardine or wool blend suit for $200 and then you wear it once a week for at least eight months of the year for three years, the cost per wearing is $2.08. You may want to run through an analysis like this before making major clothing purchases.

———— 🐘 ————

Investment dressing can stretch your budget and consists of selecting items that will work together with interchangeable fabrics. Suits are good investment items because you can separate the pieces and make several other good-looking fashions. If you add a few blouses, you can create a month's worth of outfits out of nine or ten items.

———————————— 🐘 ————————————

*If you have a low budget
for your wardrobe one season,
just add scarves and jewelry to coordinate
and update your look. This will
add interest and flair.*

Buy only those pieces that will perform in your life. A perfect example would be a tweed skirt, trousers, and a jacket with a solid silk blouse that matches perfectly. Add a silk skirt that matches the blouse which could also make it a dress. This is investment shopping.

•

Purchase two pairs of shoes in basic and neutral colors that blend with all your clothing. Purchase one in a basic pump and one in a dressier sling-back style to extend your wardrobe and pocketbook.

•

It is important to develop a sense of your own style by collecting from magazines and catalogs pictures that fit the image you want to portray such as sporty, professional, or feminine.

•

Do not limit yourself to one look and when you shop you will have an easier time finding an affordable outfit.

•

Before purchasing any more clothing, sit down and list at least three or four of your best features. Too many women only look at the things that are wrong with them, so begin to look at your good points and accent those best features. For example if you have a great waistline, then belt it. If you have really pretty eyes, then wear attractive earrings to draw attention upward. If you have pretty hands then wear a beautiful bracelet or distinctive watch to draw attention to them.

•

Be sure that you wear the proper height shoe heel when you are purchasing a garment because this small point can make a big difference in the look of your purchase.

•

It is advantageous to write down the combinations that you have made because you may forget them when they are all put away in the closet. Use your list to remind you of your new discoveries and also use it as an aid when shopping.

•

Do not be afraid to wear accessories; often they are what really pulls fashion together.

•

Colors can play a big part in investment buying. Neutrals, such as beige, gray, navy, and black, as well as white, can be worn year-round by mixing and matching. Add different colors to them for a particular season.

•

A variety of white blouses probably does not sound very exciting but they are great extenders for your wardrobe.

•

Make a note of anything you need to expand your wardrobe, such as a new belt and then you can create an entirely new ensemble by making only a minor investment.

Basic Clothing Tips
to Help You Wear What You Buy

Before you purchase another thing, think about the things in your closet that you already have. You will probably find that your favorite clothes all have a similar mood, style, or fabric. Then ask yourself why you love these items of clothing. Once you know, you can then add things to your wardrobe that you are comfortable wearing. This will keep you from making further purchase mistakes.

Make a list of clothing items that you never wear and that ended up hanging in the back of your closet. Analyze those mistakes so that you are less prone to buying unwisely again.

------ &. ------

Many of us have trouble finding slacks that fit properly. We need to make sure that they fit in the hips and the rise. Bend and sit in them to see if they are comfortable. Never buy slacks (or any garment for that matter) that are too tight and then plan to let them out later.

•

An outfit looks better if it does not wrinkle too much. An outfit is a good buy if it requires a minimum amount of care.

•

Buy clothing that gives you freedom of movement.

•

Another thing to consider when you purchase something is to ask yourself if you are wearing the garment or if it is wearing you.

•

Going for the look of quality instead of quantity will allow you to buy good clothes that you can wear year after year without wearing them out. Some traditional clothes stay in fashion forever so it is more practical to spend money on garments that will stay in style at least long enough to stabilize your wardrobe.

•

When you purchase clothing keep in mind the upkeep of the garment because sometimes your dry cleaning bills can run you almost as much as the cost of the garment. If you have a garment that is made out of a washable fabric with a label that says "Dry clean only," be sure that you dry clean it.

•

Cheaper clothing does tend to be cut somewhat smaller so although you might wear a size eight in a higher-priced garment, you may have to buy a ten or twelve in the cheaper brand. Judge your true size by the medium-priced clothing because in the less expensive garments you will generally be one size larger.

•

Learn to mix the two worlds of work and nonwork clothes and you may find that they may go together to expand your wardrobe with different layering.

•

It is easier to pull pieces together if you stay within one theme or type of fashion. Funky clothing does not fit well into a closet of classics.

•

An elegantly dressed woman knows that simplicity is a dramatic fashion statement.

Coat Purchases

A coat with a classic shape is an investment and you will wear it with joy year after year. Buy the best that you can afford, and this means the best in fabric, workmanship, and fit, and you will have a coat that will give you the longest life.

No coat will meet all of your needs from a pair of jeans to an evening look. Therefore, carefully think about your purchase and buy a coat that will go the farthest in your wardrobe.

———— ✌ ————

A good basic coat for year-round use would be the classic trenchcoat. Simple is best in a coat purchase.

•

The ideal lining for a raincoat will button or zip out, making the coat seasonless from winter to spring.

•

Too much detail on a coat will limit its use as well as make the look too complicated and sometimes bulky. Some examples of overdetailing could be big fancy buttons, too many buttons, too many yokes, too much stitching, and multitudes of pocket flaps with decorations. Sometimes the manufacturer gives you your money's worth by adding accessories but this is not necessarily the best look.

The length of the coat should cover the hem of your garment by at least a half-inch. The exception being of course the three-quarter-length coat which comes to about mid-thigh.

The sleeve length is very important because a sleeve that is too short will make the coat look as if it is too small.

Check the fit of the collar and shoulder to see that the coat hangs evenly, comfortably and straight and make sure that it does not feel heavy across the shoulders. Heaviness across the shoulders can cause pain after hours of wearing and it is a sign that something is wrong with the fit.

Comfort should be a number one priority in a coat. Raise your arms to make sure that you do not feel any resistance.

Consider carefully what you will be wearing under your coat. If you wear a lot of jackets, a cape may be a good purchase for you because it fits very comfortably over suits and jackets.

If you wear a lot of jackets, try your coat on over the jacket to test for comfort.

•

If you mainly wear your coat over blouses, dresses or sweaters, then the coat should fit more like a jacket or it will look too large.

———————

If you want to choose a coat that goes from daytime to evening, then choose a black, simple-line, wool-blend, dress-length coat. You can add beautiful mufflers and brooches to the collar in the daytime or add soft flowing scarves for evening. This purchase would be a good investment and would always look classy. Coats can be a major purchase so it is best to spend a little more and be able to wear it comfortably for years. A plain color is better than a plaid because it is dressier and will go with more things in your wardrobe. A neutral color like beige, black, or navy will coordinate with almost anything. A hot pink coat may be pretty but it will definitely be harder to work into your wardrobe.

PART 5

Women's Clothes

Knowing What to Wear

She is clothed with strength and dignity.
—Proverbs 31:25

When we feel good about ourselves and know that we are put together properly, then we can forget ourselves and give to another person. That is what truly makes us beautiful.

So many women want to add something special to their rather dull and drab fashion selections but they do not know where to start so they do nothing. Hopefully this book has given you some knowledge and confidence so that you will be able to spend your money for something you know will work in your present wardrobe. It is fun and exciting to go up the ladder of fashion and improve yourself in some way especially when you have some idea what to do.

Developing a professional image will vary depending on your job, position, where you live, and your company's dress code. However, never dress down to look more dowdy and dull. Be a leader in looking professional. Recent studies have revealed that women who wear slacks to work regularly remain in the secretarial pool longer than those who dress up in skirts and coordinated jackets.

Professional Dress and Coordination

Buy basics and separates that will move from one look into another, so you can have a multitude of looks year after year by simply adding a new blouse, new belt, or a variety of other accessories. The cost becomes considerably less than buying a completely new outfit every year.

•

Always purchase your first suits in neutral and basic colors to blend in your wardrobe. A navy suit will go a lot further and look more professional than a purple one. For instance, in the business world, choose a three-piece suit in your best dark basic, a second suit in your best light neutral, and a third suit in one of your best coordinating colors. This will give you a workable, interchangeable, coordinated beginning.

•

The next purchase should be a pretty skirt and blouse that match and can be worn together to look like a dress. As separates these will also be wearable in so many different ways. It is best to get them in a subtle and interesting color that you are working with in your wardrobe and then purchase a soft sweater and some nice slacks in a complimentary color. Then you will have four pieces to mix and match with endless variety.

•

Another good coordination idea is to get one suit in a neutral color such as blue, navy, or gray and then add the other one in a small muted plaid or tweed. Then you can go from office to dinner meetings with a minimum change.

•

Choose complimentary fabrics and styles so that you can mix jackets and skirts. If you have a dress or a couple of basic skirts in coordinating colors, it will help to expand your wardrobe.

•

Choose a fabric that can be worn year-round and will go with a multitude of fabrics to get the most for your money. Some good examples are wool blends, gabardine, natural silk, and some silk blends and some polyester blends. Do not get polyester knit. The gabardine look has proven to be the best fabric for year-round wearing and moves very nicely into dresses and other combinations. Pure linen suits wrinkle badly.

———————

Although a good suit or a fashion look with a jacket is essential for an executive, many of the other jobs in the office may allow for a more casual look. It has been suggested, however, that you should dress for the job you want, not the job you have.

Study the fashion magazines for help in putting together a good suited look. Look around your office and get some tips from those who dress in a way that you admire. You do not have to copy but learn some good ways to put a professional look together as well as what to avoid.

———— ❧ ————

If you need a suit, look for fabrics that are not stiff or shiny.

———————————————— ❧ ————————————————

Choose a suit that is simple. Avoid the cluttered look of extra pockets, flaps, or extra buttons.

———————————————————————————

When buying a suit, the inside should look as well-made as the outside. Look for quality finishing and make sure there are no loose threads or raw edges showing.

•

Top stitching on a jacket should be the same color as the suit for maximum versatility.

•

Look for the sleek and classic lines.

•

Use your own personal touches and personality to jazz up a suit.

•

A lace jabot (lace down the front of a blouse added for extra running softness) used with an old-fashioned cameo pin at the neck will add a very feminine touch.

•

If your figure can handle belts, try belting the jacket on the outside.

•

In the workplace, it is important not to wear any sheer, see-through fabrics, clinging styles, and, of course, no outfits so small that you burst the seams. Also, save the more casual things for leisure time, vacation, and evening.

•

Do not wear jangling charm bracelets or long, dangling earrings to the office. Many business advisors still frown on ankle chains or bracelets. Exceptions to this rule would be people in the fashion industry.

Remember, your clothing affects your own moods as well as the moods of those people looking at you. It is interesting to note that when you wear a more business look your language tends to follow your image and when you are wearing casual clothes your language tends to become more casual. It has been shown that if you stay home on a drizzling afternoon to write a letter and you wear a crisp, clean blouse and slacks, your letter will reflect a different mood than if you are all bundled up in something warm and cozy. Be aware of how a change of clothing can affect you. For example, when you take off an apron, does it change your mood?

The message that you convey with your clothing should harmonize and enhance your personality. When people look at you, they are not looking to see if you are thicker in the waist than you should be or if you are wearing last season's style. What they like to see when they look at a person is a harmonious image. People read the messages your clothing sends, and if you look like one of the employees when you are actually the boss, some of your credibility with people may be lost.

If you develop a consistency of taste and image then you will find that your wardrobe will begin to expand itself with many changes. In the beginning you will have to think every match through very carefully rather than having the luxury of it just happening.

—— 🙠 ——

A good basic rule is to mix one expensive, quality item with something of lesser quality.

•

Another good idea is to wear the most expensive item near your face.

•

You can usually get away with a less expensive skirt if it fits well because most people do not study a skirt when you are seated or moving. However, the superior look in a fabric or the unique tailoring in a blouse or jacket will enhance your image.

•

One thing that can make a blouse look expensive is the fine detail it may have on the collar and cuffs.

•

Always check the sleeve length of a jacket carefully. A jacket or coat sleeve should be just long enough to cover the top of the wrist bone letting your blouse cuff peek out a quarter of an inch.

More Hints for Business Dressing

If you have suits in your closet that you just don't seem to be getting maximum use of, try the suit jackets with different skirts and pants, checking out all possible combinations. (Your closet has to be cleaned out before you can do this effectively.)

—— 🙠 ——

Dresses are being worn more now than in the past so a nice tailored dress in gabardine or jersey with soft shoulder padding could be a good option.

•

Unmatched suits with a mixture of textures are very fashionable and a good way to extend your wardrobe.

•

The color pink is acceptable in a blouse in the business world, but does not seem to be as professional in a suit. The experts say that it does not show enough authority. However, the muted mauve pink and muted fuchsia colors lend quality to the look of a garment. The powder pink or shocking pink do not seem to be as good.

•

Your overall presentation including a briefcase, handbag, and shoes should show quality to maintain an image in the business world.

Do not forget to add some vests to your wardrobe. You will be surprised at how a vest can totally make a dull drab outfit look very special.

To go to an after-dinner business meeting, wear your basic suit skirt and add a softer cardigan knit sweater and some nice pearls. You could also complete a nice evening look with a pair of colored hosiery and a dressier pair of shoes.

•

The high rubber wedge shoe or dressy shoe with straps is not a professional shoe.

Women's Jackets

If you have a limited budget, the best purchase for your wardrobe would be a new jacket. It will be the most important and most expensive thing you buy so make it the highest quality you can afford. If you do not work outside the home, it can be an important item in your wardrobe for meetings, church, etc.

When purchasing a jacket be sure that it is versatile and will go over several different shirts, slacks, and dresses in your wardrobe.

•

Buy a solid-colored jacket to go with most of your tweed or patterned skirts and pants. Then buy another jacket with a different shape in a pattern like a subtle tweed or plaid to go with the other half of your wardrobe—the skirts and pants that are solid. This makes it easy to stay within two color families that are compatible and you can intermix and always be able to finish the look of each outfit with a jacket.

•

Jackets are an important item of clothing to have in your wardrobe. When you have an interview they can add presence to you as a person and they can add credibility for you in meetings or in the presentation of a speech. A jacket gives upper body presence.

•

Some types of jackets to consider are the tailored look, the cardigan which falls straight without buttons, the easy shirt jacket, and the blouson jacket. The blouson jacket is usually bloused over the derriere in a longer style which is good for many figures.

Dressy Clothes

Simplicity is an elegant look and the feeling of being fashionable can be achieved through the wise choice of fabric, color, and design when you are choosing a party dress.

——— ❧ ———

Some dressy fabrics are silks, satins, panne velvet, lace, and subtle metallic in black and gold.

•

If you can wear black, it always makes an elegant evening ensemble.

•

You can take a good pair of wool crepe slacks, wear them sporty in the day with a tweed blazer and then just change to a gold-flecked blouse and metallic belt to make them more dressy for the evening.

•

Another suggestion for evening would be a skirt that is soft, narrow, and ankle length with a soft tunic top, beautiful blouse, or even a camisole and small quilted jacket. These tops could also be worn with a soft silk pajama pant for a completely different look.

•

Evening wear separates are more versatile than a dress or gown that has only one look. When money is an issue, versatility is a key word.

•

Whenever you are shopping, keep your eyes open for clothing pieces that can be made more formal. When you do this, you will save money because dressier clothes are more expensive.

•

No matter how elegant and beautiful an outfit is, you will not feel confident in it if it is not appropriate for the occasion. Take the time to find out from your hostess what kind of dress or ensemble to wear.

Clothing is not the most important thing in the world, but it has been said that when we are well-dressed we have a calmer feeling about ourselves and our surroundings.

Some General Clothing Tips

If a metal zipper becomes stuck, try rubbing the point of a lead pencil over it. You can rub a cake of soap across the face of a plastic zipper for the same results.

•

Dab transparent nail polish on the centers of sewed-on buttons. This seals the thread and prevents unraveling.

•

Rub a fresh fabric softener sheet over your slip and stockings to prevent dresses from clinging.

•

To help eliminate static cling try running a wire coat hanger between your dress and your slip to draw out the static electricity.

•

Another way to eliminate cling is to starch your slips.

•

If you will hang what you are planning to wear in the bath-room while you take a shower, the steam will seep into the fabric and eliminate static.

•

If your fur gets wet, shake gently to remove excess moisture, then hang on a sturdy wooden hanger in a well-ventilated area away from the heat.

•

If you have accidentally washed a wool garment in water that is too hot, soak it in tepid water with a couple of capfuls of good shampoo to soften the wool. Then reshape and block.

•

Get rid of ugly pilling on sweaters by laying the fabric on a hard surface and lightly shaving the garment with a razor. Be sure the fabric is dry and shave with the grain of the fabric.

•

Rub white vinegar onto underarm perspiration stains with a white cloth and wash as usual. This is a good way to take both stain and odor out.

CHAPTER

18

Accessories That Make a Difference

She is clothed in fine linen and purple.
—Proverbs 31:22

Accessories refer to everything except the main garment Poor accessories can make a very classy outfit look cheap, so be a collector of good accessories and choose them for how long they will last. When choosing accessories, choose ones that harmonize with each other and can be worn with more than one outfit. Also, purchase all accessories with your personality in mind.

Accessories play an important role in your plan to dress fashionably and can help you get maximum mileage from a small, compact wardrobe as well as provide new life for old classics.

—————— 🐚 ——————

Too many accessories or points of interest will cheapen the whole look so strive for simplicity. However, most people underaccessorize.

•

It is fun to keep up with the changing fads, but invest the most money in the classics such as good jewelry and good leather.

•

Remember that a bolder accessory at the waist means less accessorizing at the neck

•

Pretty sweaters sometimes look even more beautiful when an antique collar is added. Also, adding new lace collars and cuffs to a blouse or sweater you already own is a very pretty update.

•

To dress down a suit add some sporty earrings.

•

To dress up a suit, button it up, leave the blouse off, and wear some jewelry that has a little more sparkle. This could go into evening very easily.

•

If you have a very mundane sweater or blouse, try accessorizing with a different type of button that may give it an entirely different look. You could make it sporty this way or more dressy.

•

If your skirt is a bit on the short side and you feel uncomfortable in it, try wearing stockings of the same color. This will make the skirt look longer.

•

You can update your blouses, dresses, and suits by adding shoulder pads.

•

A blouse and a skirt that are different colors can be turned into an interesting outfit by adding a scarf or a shawl that has the same two colors in its print.

•

Do not clutter an elegant look with too bright an accent in a scarf or jewelry.

•

The color of an accessory can either coordinate with an outfit or it can add a neat look of contrast. For example, a blue knit dress, soft blue-tinted hose, and blue shoes might be boring. To be more exciting try wearing a bright, contrasting color at the waist or neck.

•

Vary your blouses with suits that have V necklines and soft bows at the neck.

•

If you want to wear the latest fashion touch such as a vest, then do not also wear the latest hat, latest stockings, latest stick pin, etc.

•

Stand in front of a full-length mirror and notice what is catching your eye the most. This can give you lots of ideas on correct accessorizing.

•

When you are adding an accent such as a collar, cuffs, yokes, and insets to an outfit, experiment with mixes of florals, plaids, and stripes.

•

Consider wearing a beautiful silk shirt over another silk blouse using it as a type of jacket.

•

One rule you will hear from the experts is to put on all the accessories that you want to wear and then take one off. It is better to have too few than too many.

•

Update your clothes by wearing them differently than you have in the past. For example, shove the sleeves up your arm for a new look from the neatly folded and cuffed style. Also, try rolling up the sleeves to just below your elbow and turn up your collar.

•

T-shirts are a classic but to change the look, knot them in the front or wear as one layer under a blouse or dress.

•

If pants are shorter for this season, then simply take up the hem a few inches and you have the new season look.

•

If you buy an outfit that has a seasonless fabric then you can wear it with western boots in the fall or with sandals in the spring.

●

Take a vest that you bought with a three-piece suit and wear it with other things.

●

You can have the look of something new by adding the latest colors to your wardrobe in small doses such as a red scarf or orange belt. Fashion magazines will clue you into the latest color hues of the season.

It is important to keep your accessories in proportion and size to the silhouette of your outfit.

A good rule of thumb is that any color in an accessory should be balanced by one more touch of that same color in another accessory. However, when you get too many color touches it can take away the balance, such as a red handbag, red shoes, red scarf, and red belt.

●

Use accessories to play up your good points and play down your bad points. For example, if your waistline is not your best asset, then do not use waist accessories.

●

To give a sweater a different look, wear a pullover sweater on the outside and belt it for a change.

●

When adding a men's tie accessory to a blouse, keep it from looking too masculine by not tying it too close to the neck and letting the tie drop down a bit in a softer knot.

●

In wearing the tie look, choose a paisley print and add a strand or two of pearls draped over the top.

•

A sweater dress is a fun item of clothing to accessorize. Instead of the same old look with delicate chains and self-belts, try adding a more dramatic look with a beautiful burnished copper belt.

•

Add beautiful, bold-looking gold and silver jewelry to your wardrobe in necklaces, earrings, and bracelets.

•

Try a new look with a blazer-type or cable-knit sweater jacket. Try adding a tweed one and update it with slight shoulder padding.

•

Add one of the large multicolored scarves or shawls and drape over your shoulder or use as a hip wrap.

•

Try adding some classy belts to some of your slacks. If your waist can take it, choose a wide belt made of interesting material like snake skin or suede.

•

Try a cummerbund with a braided overbelt in a contrasting color.

•

Silk dresses are fun to accessorize. Perk one up with a pretty sweater vest. Be sure that you match the color of the vest with the color of the dress.

•

Change the look of some of your older clothes by adding new fashionable buttons.

•

To get contrast in an outfit, add a collar and cuffs using creative fabric combinations such as contrasting fabric and luster in the material.

———————

Work on some new tricks by experimenting with various looks and come up with your own signature style. An example might be to work on slight switches in jewelry and scarves which can make many outfits look very different.

Accessories are like the icing on a cake because they add sparkle and interest to clothes that would otherwise be "just a dress" or "just a blouse." They change a look from day to evening or from winter to summer. They are an inexpensive way for you to update your clothing into the new looks of the season without making major purchases.

Start with the Handbag

Handbags are a very important accessory and oftentimes reflect our personality. It is important to buy handbags that add to your image rather than subtract. Your handbag should be a pleasure to carry and should make your life easier when you use it.

——— ❧ ———

Choose a neutral color that will blend with many pairs of shoes in your closet.

•

Nothing can downgrade a nice outfit faster than a shoddy handbag. Handbags should be of top quality and they can be one of your most expensive purchases. However, in the long run a good handbag will give you many years of excellent service. Buy leather handbags. Vinyl bags do not last very long and will not give you your full money's worth. One exception to buying leather might be if you have an odd color outfit and you will be using the vinyl bag only as a coordination piece. However, your everyday and frequently used bags need to be leather. Leather improves as it gets older and will last much longer as well as look much better.

•

Bags and shoes do not have to match exactly but they should be in blendable or complimentary tones.

•

Be sure that the handbag has a good zipper or clasp.

•

Test a handbag before you buy it. Will it hold everything you need to carry all day and does it have compartments to make your life easier? There is nothing worse than when you leave home and you find that your compact or glasses won't fit in the handbag you have chosen for the day or when the bag causes you to lose everything at the bottom.

•

Does the bag feel comfortable on your shoulder?

•

Look for a handbag with gussets that expand.

Keep in mind that when you change to an evening look, you need to change to a handbag that is smaller and less cluttered. A small clutch would be a good investment.

Can you see in it easily and are frequently needed items such as keys in an accessible place? Be aware that some key rings will scratch things in your bag.

•

Keep keys in a brightly colored eyeglass case. Even though you may have a special place for them in the bag, sometimes you can get in a hurry and forget, but when you use a case it helps keep them handy. A spare eyeglass case also makes a great holder for a small hairbrush and comb. Another good idea is to use an eyeglass case as a holder for pens and pencils to avoid unwanted marks on your wallet and the inside lining of your handbag.

•

Be sure that you do not overfill shoulder bags. This could cause you to pull yourself out of good body alignment causing many backaches.

•

Do not stuff evening bags so full that they bulge for this takes away from the elegant look you want to create for evening. For the evening carry only the essentials like a handkerchief, some small change, and some keys.

•

Do not carry a short strap bag like a suitcase; instead put it through the arm and place it in front of the body.

•

Clutch bags are carried high up under the arm with most of the bag forward. The profile of the hand should hold the bag firmly in the front.

•

Think proportion when buying a handbag. Small women carry small bags, medium women carry medium handbags, etc.

Scarves and Shawls

When adding important accessories of the season to your wardrobe you will discover that scarves are always a good purchase. Add an accessory such as a scarf to your wardrobe to blend into last year's closet of clothes. It can also be used as an accent near the face when something that you have purchased is not the best color for you. Scarves can be a great addition to your wardrobe if they are well chosen.

——— ❧ ———

Large geometric scarves and shawls add interest to a wardrobe. Taller women can wear the much larger scarf and larger print. Everyone can wear scarves regardless of age or size if they are worn in the correct manner. Just keep your proportions in mind and where you want the accent

•

Check for proportion when you look in the mirror. See if the scarf makes you look top-heavy.

•

The shorter you are the smaller the scarf.

•

Silk is the best fabric for tying. A silk square looks very good tied and neatly tucked into a sweater. Fabrics such as silk, crepe de chine, and cashmere are always good buys and make an outfit look more expensive.

•

If you have a high neckline, a scarf can work well tied around the outside of a collar and knotted.

•

Long cashmere scarves are a good accessory with coats and jackets.

•

Shawls can be a real asset to the larger figured woman with large hips because they can be used as an attractive camouflage. Oprah Winfrey uses this look very effectively.

•

Collect both solids and prints and remember that the small menswear tie designs on silk scarves always look great for business

•

Look for little checks or flowers on silk or cotton scarves for summertime.

•

Larger flowers and prints work best on larger scarves. Usually the rule to follow is the smaller the scarf the smaller the print or pattern

•

Be sure to look for hand-rolled or machine-rolled edges on the scarves.

•

If the edges are fringed, they should be at least a half inch deep on silk scarves and shawls, and even deeper on wool. The finish on a scarf or shawl is very important

•

Do not hesitate to mix gold and silver jewelry and pearls with the scarf or shawl to give an entirely new fashion touch.

•

Some of the smaller scarves can be used as a pocket accent by letting them drape over the top of the pocket like a pretty handkerchief. Be sure that your bustline can take this accent.

•

A very tailored shirt can be brightened and made more feminine with a soft grosgrain ribbon tied into a bow at the top of the collar or with an attractive coordinated scarf tied in a bow.

*A shawl can also be tied
sarong style around your top to make
an instant exotic blouse.
Add a bright jacket and you have
a brand-new look.*

One of the secrets to wearing a scarf is having it secured to your garment. To keep your scarf in place use pins underneath that do not show or fasten it with a beautiful brooch. The only way that a scarf or shawl looks good is if it looks effortless and natural. Otherwise do not wear it.

•

Even if you have a short neck you can wear a scarf, just do not tie it too close to your neck and try to keep the fabric soft and not too bulky.

•

Try using a long multicolored scarf sashed around your waist to add color during the day and then switch to a softer printed silk scarf for evening, adding some dressy jewelry.

•

Sling a shawl or large scarf over your shoulder and belt it in place at your waist. This looks good with slacks as well as skirts and dresses.

•

Always carefully remove the label from a scarf before wearing it.

It is important for you to not be afraid to use these items to accessorize since they add pizzazz for not too much money. For example, a basic dress can go from morning to evening simply by adding a clever scarf accessory.

Scarves are a great way to accent a pretty neck as well as enhance your face. You can bring your best colors up to your face and create some softness. Don't be concerned about how to tie a scarf. There are many little books you can pick up in most department stores and the illustrations are simple and easy to use.

Belts

Belts are good purchases if your waist is one of your assets since they add a very simple, classic, and fashionable touch to your wardrobe. A rule of thumb when purchasing a belt is that it must be of excellent quality. You are much better off with fewer belts of better quality, such as leather, than many cheap ones.

——— ❧ ———

You can change a moderately priced dress that comes with a self-tie belt (which tends to downgrade the look immediately) from chintzy to classy by simply adding a neat-looking belt.

•

Generally speaking, belts should be purchased in varying shades of neutrals and basics. Tans and natural leather for instance blend very nicely while belts in contrasting colors can be effective but they will also give more emphasis to the waistline.

•

If you are an ardent belt wearer, wonderful interchangeable belt buckles are worth considering.

•

If you want to blouse a top or dress over a belt, before belting lift your shoulders as high as possible, and while your shoulders are lifted, belt. You then have an even excess of fabric about the belt so then when you relax your shoulders you will have the perfectly bloused amount.

•

Think of a suit like a dress and add fashion touches such as belts and lapel pins. A good belt finishes the look of a suit or skirt.

•

A good purchase would be a one-half to three-quarter-inch wide belt in a neutral color to wear with skirts and pants when the blouse is tucked in.

•

For a dressier look you might like to add a gold or silver belt.

•

Use your imagination to create unusual and striking belts such as winding scarves around your waist.

•

If your waist cannot take a belted look, then use a skinny belt in metal with a smaller belt buckle, which could peep out from under a vest or a jacket.

•

A soft leather free-form belt is a fun accessory that you can tie in many different ways.

Nylons

Maybe you have never considered hosiery an accessory, but it can be one of the most interesting accessories that you wear and it can add a real fashion touch to your wardrobe.

——— ❧ ———

Change the look of your entire outfit by adding a new pair of textured hosiery. Women with shapely legs can wear the pinstripes, tweeds, and herringbone hosiery.

•

When wearing boots, try to match your hose color to your boot to prevent too many breaks in the line.

●

Blend your nylon into your shoe for the best elongated and non-choppy look. If you wear black hosiery with black shoes, it will give you a longer and taller line.

●

If in doubt on a hosiery color, wear taupe for cool colors and suntan for warm colors. The fashion industry breaks this rule with some fad fashions by putting white nylons with a black or navy shoe. Unless you have a nicely shaped leg this is not the best look for you. Remember the eye goes to the lightest or brightest thing on your body first.

---

*Darker shades of hosiery
will diminish heavier legs.*

When you wear neutral-tone hosiery, it will make your legs look slightly tanned.

●

A wool-like, textured stocking that is the same color as your outfit makes your outfit look sporty. Opaque navy hose with a navy skirt and sweater is a good example.

●

Picking up a minor color in your outfit with your hosiery does not work well.

●

Do not wear the reinforced-toe nylons with open-toed shoes.

●

To help your panty hose last longer, try adding a few drops of liquid fabric softener to the final rinse water.

●

Nylon is strengthened from cold so rinse your hose in ice water, dry them, and then store them in your freezer and they will last much longer.

•

Buy at least two pair of the same color of hosiery; then when a run does occur you can cut off the leg of the one that has the run. Do the same with the extra pair when it gets a run and then you will still have one good pair with extra support over the tummy.

Shoes

Shoes are an accessory that makes a big difference not only in adding to your fashion wardrobe but in adding to the attractiveness of the leg. Shoes can make or break an outfit. If you wear a perfectly coordinated dress or suit with run-down shoes, it can ruin the entire look. Shoes should never make the statement of an outfit but should add to the elegance of an outfit.

——— ❧ ———

Unless you want someone to look at your feet first, do not wear a shoe lighter than the hem of your garment such as a white shoe with a navy skirt. A brighter shoe such as red is a nice accent.

•

Shoes with slingback heels that show more foot make the leg appear younger than closed pumps. A lighter weight, higher pump is a younger look than the heavy, low pump. The Chanel two-toned slingback shoe is a wonderful classic and always looks smart. This would be a great choice for a second pair of shoes.

•

Low-cut pumps or low-cut slingbacks with narrow, medium-height heels are very flattering for most women and are best bets for an everyday shoe. A low-cut shallow shoe interferes very little with the line of the leg and gives it a long slim look. The pump should be made of the finest calfskin. You will get a lot of mileage out of this shoe. Fine leather pumps are perfect for any season and are adaptable to any time of the day. For business wear, the classic pump is probably the best choice.

•

In buying shoes you can minimize the ankles and slenderize the calves if you avoid ankle straps and pick a pointed toe.

•

Your feet will appear slimmer if your shoes are all one color and cut low.

•

If you want your ankles to look larger, then wear ankle straps, rounded or square toes, two-toned shoes, buckles, or bows and you will add width.

•

In general, the less shoe there is the better the leg will appear.

•

In choosing a shoe, remember proportion in heel height. Generally, the longer the skirt the higher the heel.

•

Suede or patent leather are very beautiful but they are not as versatile and would be a better buy as a second or third pair of shoes.

•

An exception to the basic or neutral shoe would be a pair of casual shoes like a purple or red sandal.

•

White shoes tend to make the foot look larger so bone or taupe would be a better choice for your wardrobe. White looks best with white outfits.

•

Shoes should be clean and well polished with the heels in good repair. Have your shoe repairer put nylon caps on the heels.

•

To protect the heels of your shoes when driving, you can purchase a heel protector to rest your heel in. Or you can wear an old pair of shoes to drive in and put your good shoes on when you reach your destination. This will prevent those rubbing marks that you get on the back of your heel.

•

Add interesting little shoe accessories and change the look of the whole shoe.

•

To make a more masculine shoe look more feminine, wear crocheted or laces-topped socks with them. This is a good tip for the younger person.

Patent leather will shine like new after a quick wipe with Windex.

Do not wear a strappy sandal with a tweed suit or a broad heeled pump with a dressy dress. If you add the wrong shoe to your outfit as well as the wrong handbag, jewelry, or belt, it makes for a very confusing fashion picture.

•

For a dressy evening occasion, a simple but elegant slingback strappy sandal will almost always look good.

•

To prevent slipping and sliding in a new pair of shoes, rub the soles with a piece of fine sandpaper to provide some traction.

•

This is a natural healing tip: Hasten and soothe the healing of blisters on your feet by rubbing them with clean, fresh-cut grass. Another natural healing tip is to purchase an aloe vera plant, break a leaf, and use the healing substance inside to rub on blisters or burns.

•

If you will toss a sheet of fabric softener into your shoes when you store them, it will cut the odor.

It is important that the shoe you purchase looks good on your feet, complements your leg, is comfortable, and works well proportionately with your body and outfit. Well-designed shoes are often high priced but worth the money for the overall effect they produce.

Some higher heeled shoes look wonderful in the store but are impossible to walk in. Do not be tempted by the look alone because if your walk or posture is affected by a hard-to-walk-in shoe, it will affect your whole fashion picture.

Boots

Boots can be a fun but also expensive accessory. They look very smart with longer skirts and with fall and winter coats. Do not wear them indoors, however, unless they are part of the overall look you are wearing.

When you wear skirts or dresses, boots add an extra dimension to your legs. However, be very careful that they do not cause extra horizontal cutting lines by showing leg between boot and hem. If your boots are a shorter cut keep your hosiery the same color as your boot. Try to avoid a space between the top of your boot and your hemline because it will tend to shorten your leg

•

Sporty boots do not look good with stylish, dressy ensembles Usually boots do not look good with silk dresses because they appear too heavy and make the fashion look unbalanced.

•

Boots are very expensive so do not buy a trendy boot that will soon be out of style. A classic style with a one- or two-inch heel would be the best buy

•

The silhouette of a boot should be slim and flattering to the leg

•

Like a good handbag, a boot should be made of the finest leather. Boots are one place you cannot skimp and still have them keep their shape and attractive look.

The color you choose for your boot should be your best dark basic that you are coordinating with. It should blend with your wardrobe and your coat. You can see how important it is for you to be coordinated throughout your wardrobe to get the most mileage from your clothes and shoes.

Pearls

Pearls are one of the best pieces of jewelry that you can purchase. Even if you do not like to wear a lot of jewelry, a string of pearls is a wonderful addition to a wardrobe and adds a touch of femininity. They are one of those time-tested purchases that will last year after year and never be out-of-date. The real ones are very nice but also very expensive. There are a lot of very good ones on the market that are not real and will serve you just as well.

If you have some pearls and wish to restore the shine then gently rub them with a little olive oil and wipe them with a soft cloth.

•

Be sure you do not get anything on your pearls that has alcohol in it. One example would be perfume which would damage the pearls.

•

Ropes of pearls can be used in multiples or mixed with other jewelry pieces.

•

The color of pearls that go best with the various color keys are rose, soft white, and gray for winter and summer people and yellow hue or cream color for spring and autumn people.

Jewelry

—— ❧ ——

Do not ever attempt to pierce your ears yourself or have a friend pierce them for you because chances are the instrument will not be sterile and you will risk infection. Ear piercing is not recommended for skin that forms keloids (hard, raised scar tissue).

•

Do not throw out any jewelry because eventually it will come back in style and you will be able to use it again. A good example of this is when the rhinestones of the past came back as a strong fashion statement in 1986 and 1991.

—————— ❧ ——————

Your watch is an important fashion accessory because you wear it every day. Since it will be noticed a lot, make sure it is a sleek, high-quality item.

Cool season people look better in silver, white gold, and rose gold jewelry and warm season people look best in yellow gold jewelry. If you have pieces that are out of your best color key, just add a few pieces of the opposite metal and wear them together. Try mixing your gold and silver chains and bracelets.

•

A sporty watch does not look good with a high-fashion dress or a business suit. If you can only purchase one watch buy a medium-sized semi-dressy watch with a gold and silver band. This will make the watch very versatile.

•

When selecting jewelry, scale it to the size of the individual. Dainty jewelry worn on a larger woman tends to get lost and a large a piece of jewelry may overpower the smaller individual.

•

A simple loop earring is very basic and works well for those with small-boned facial features; the smaller the circumference of the earring the thicker it can be. The larger the circumference, the thinner it should be.

•

Rings are fun and should be scaled to the size of the hand and worn appropriately for the occasion. Since rings draw attention to your hand, it is important to have your nails well manicured.

•

When leading a meeting or speaking in public, be sure that your jewelry does not move or make noise. Bracelets are a nice fashion choice and add a touch of pizzazz to any outfit, but they can be very distracting if they jingle.

•

Jewelry for dressier occasions should sparkle or be made of gold and silver.

•

Wear only two pieces of matched jewelry at one time and remember that cleverly combined jewelry can create a very chic look.

•

Brushed metal is very dressy especially when used with stones and pearls.

•

Shiny metal is used frequently for the sporty and casual look, although there are a lot of shiny metal pieces that are elegant for evening.

•

Shiny and brushed metals are combined for a less dressy look.

•

Plastic, wood, ceramic, shell, and leather jewelry is very casual and should be worn with natural cottons and more casual fabrics.

•

Do not forget to use lapel pins at the neckline of a blouse or dress or on a lapel to add a fresh fashion touch.

•

Avoid using too much gaudy jewelry. Gaudy jewelry looks best on younger women and usually is worn with casual or sporty clothes.

•

Have a jeweler convert an unused ring or pin into a choker necklace. This is a good way to put to use a precious piece of jewelry that is seldom worn.

Gloves

Gloves are usually purchased to keep the hands warm and clean but they are no longer used for just that purpose. They can be worn to add another dimension of fashion to your outfit.

———— ❧ ————

A good basic glove is made of cloth or leather and should be neutral in color.

•

When a person wears white gloves the hands become the focal point of the outfit.

•

The best length for a glove is a short glove that covers the wrist bone.

Glasses

Do not be concerned if you have to start wearing glasses. Today there are shapes and colors for every face and coloring and there are styles for all activities. Consider your lifestyle when choosing a glass frame. Whether your style is high-fashion, preppy, or classic, there are flattering eyeglasses to give you the look you desire.

Many people do not like to wear glasses, and do not realize the effect those glasses can produce. For example, a business-like frame can make a young woman look more mature and authoritative.

Frames

The shape of your face and the coloring of your skin should be considered when choosing frames. A proper frame should reflect your lifestyle, primary wardrobe colors, and personal preference.

Before you purchase a frame, determine your face shape by pulling your hair away from your face and study the outline from your temple to jawline. Ask yourself if you see curves or straight lines. Curves suggest a round or heart-shaped face and straight lines suggest an oblong or square face. Also check your proportion—width and length—and then choose frames that contrast with your facial shape. Do not repeat your face shape with the shape of the frame. Another way to determine your face shape is by drawing an outline of your face on a mirror with a tube of lipstick or a bar of soap. Step away and you will see where your face is wide or narrow. This will give you a pretty good idea of your face shape.

The eyewear you choose should be properly proportioned for the size and shape of your face. If your frame is too big, you will look out of proportion or if your frame is too small, it will make you look closed in, both in eyes and face shape. A rule for frames is that they should be as wide as the widest part of your face and be in proportion to the shape and size of your face.

—— 🙠 ——

When selecting eyeglasses, look at them in both the counter mirror and a full-length mirror. It is important to appraise the way glasses affect your overall silhouette.

•

Make a long face appear wider and shorter by choosing wider frames that cover a good portion of your face. A long face and an angular-shaped face can be shortened with a square or rounded shape and by choosing glasses that are gentle in shape and color.

•

The heart-shaped face looks good in the shorter rectangular frame.

•

The square face should wear frames that have soft, curving lines. If you have a square face, then choose a rounded or oval frame. Avoid repeating the square jaw with square frames.

•

Round faces look very nice when they wear frames that are deep and angular or geometrically shaped.

•

People with oval faces look good in just about any shaped frame. However, even though they can wear about any shaped frame, keep in mind the individual personality.

•

Women with larger noses should look for eyeglasses where all the fashion accents are at the side of the temples, drawing attention away from the center of the face and the nose.

•

If your eyes are set close together, choose an oval shape that widens or flattens out toward the sides and choose a color that is pale at the bridge of the nose and deepens toward the sides and outer edges.

•

If your hairstyle is full and worn close to the face, try a thinner, lighter frame.

•

Less hair worn on the face would call for a slightly bolder frame.

Eyeglasses and Color

Always select a frame in the correct color key for your skin tone. When choosing glasses, think about having a total, balanced look in color and frame. The right color brings a warm, healthy, natural glow to the face whereas the wrong color may make the complexion appear pale, sallow, flushed, or muddy. If you have had your color key done and know your skin tone, then use your best basic and neutrals to guide you in choosing a frame tint. Cool tints are the clear soft blues and grays, taupe, silver, and rose gold. The warm tints are peaches, golds, and warm browns.

—— ❧ ——

If you wear a tinted lens in your glasses be sure it is in a tone that will blend with your skin tone and makeup.

•

Rose tints add a warmth to a sallow skin but the color should always be subtle in a soft blend.

•

If your complexion is pale, do not overpower your delicate look. Try using powdered and icy pastels for cool skins and light earth-tone colors if you have a warm skin tone.

•

The rosy complexion needs to be softened so try wearing blue-cast cool colors and neutrals. Avoid the reds and the pinks.

—————————— ❧ ——————————

The darker the frame the smaller the face will appear.

The olive complexion looks best in rosy or blue-cast colors in a deep, vivid or icy shade or in the clear, bright neutrals. Avoid orange, gold, and yellow-green undertone colors as well as those with too much ashy tone.

•

Light frames make the face appear as it really is.

•

A frame with a light color placed high on the temple is good for lengthening a short face and a darker frame color placed low on the temple will shorten a long face.

•

If you have sallow skin, add a little cheek color to your face at the lower outer edge of your lenses.

•

If you prefer a metal frame, silver is best for cool skin and gold is best for warm skin. Silver is wonderful with gray or white hair.

•

When wearing tinted glasses it is important that people can see your eyes to make eye contact with you. Too much tint gives the feeling that the person is hiding.

If you do not want to wear glasses and can see at a distance but have trouble reading, one alternative is to wear a contact in one eye for reading. This takes some getting used to but it is another alternative to wearing glasses. Bifocal contacts are also a possibility.

Sunglasses

Another interesting accessory is a perfect pair of sunglasses. When buying sunglasses, look for strength, ultraviolet protection, comfort, and freedom from distortion. Sunglasses are important in high glare conditions, such as skiing where the light is very intense, or in driving conditions where the brightness may blind you to oncoming traffic.

The best tint choices for sunglasses are brown or sage green which probably give the best all-round protection. Other tints are neutral and smoky gray. All of these reduce the intensity but do not affect the values of the colors. Avoid the rosier tinted reds, pinks, yellows, and oranges.

•

In the summertime when everyone dons a pair of sunglasses, choose a pair that will flatter your face shape and add some glamour to your image.

•

Be careful to not get frames out of proportion to your face size.

Hats

Though hats are not worn often now, they always add a finishing fashion touch to an already elegant outfit. A woman's hat serves two main functions: It decorates her and adds to her sense of presence.

Hats come in every shape and color and some of the most interesting looks are the classic menswear, the safari, the pillbox, the oversized brims, and the fuller crowns. The right hat adds height and credibility to the wearer. For a man or a woman, a hat has served as a traditional symbol of power, position, and authority.

—— ❧ ——

If you are a small woman do not purchase too large a hat that will wear you instead of you wearing it. Think proportion with this accessory.

•

Many hats should be worn low on the brow and to the side. Women will often make the mistake of wearing a hat too far back on the head. It is best to adjust the hat up or down on the forehead. A forward tilt to the middle of the forehead is best.

•

Straw and linen hats are great for spring and summer but if you have a limited wardrobe budget then purchase a felt hat which can be worn all year.

•

Hats made of feathers, fur, or velvet are best for the winter months with velvet used mainly in the evening. Don't forget turbans and fancy evening hats.

•

The medium-brimmed hat and the women's medium-sized fedora tested best for hats in business. The fedora should not look masculine so attach a little feather to it to add a more feminine look.

•

It is fun to buy a classic cheaper hat, remove the trim, and then add a band of trim from the material of your dress. Presto, you have a nice, coordinated look.

•

The only time it is necessary to remove your hat is when you are attending a movie, concert, or theater performance. Take your hat off when the lights go down to avoid obstructing the view of the people behind you.

•

Hats need to be treated with respect so always handle your hat gently and delicately place it in a hatbox for storage.

•

When buying a hat, be sure to try it on in front of a full-length mirror to take into consideration your own proportions.

_____

One of the reasons that women have a hard time wearing hats is because they make such a strong statement and they cause people to look at you the minute you walk into a room. Many women do not like this extra attention, but most of the time the comments made about the woman wearing the hat are very positive.

19

Dressing Different Body Types

He wraps himself in light as with a garment.
—Psalm 104:2

There are many types of figures with different problem areas. To discover the best choices to help you meet your wardrobe needs, you need to understand clothing principles that minimize your figure problems and maximize your positive attributes. Clothing gives a definite visual message. It is an expression of your personality from which your emotions, attitudes, interests, and values emanate.

Knowing your proportion and best design in clothing should be one of your top considerations in making wise wardrobe decisions. It is important to flatter your figure with shape, texture, and line. The following tips will give you a good guide on do's and don'ts for different figure problems.

Full-Figured Fashion Tips

Start by getting a clear view of your problem areas. Have pictures of yourself from the front, back, and side view in some of your most-often-worn outfits. This will help you develop a critical eye from angles you usually do not see. Many people do not realize the importance of line in dressing. Lines can make you look taller, slimmer, shorter, or heavier.

General Tips for the Full-Figured Body

——— ❧ ———

Shawl collars, A-line shapes, Empire waistlines, and V-necklines create the illusion of length and will make you look thinner.

•

Wear a chemise and a dropped waist to extend a slim look.

•

Avoid too much trim. If you do have trim on a garment, be sure that it is vertical.

•

Do not add bulk to an outfit. Wear sleeveless blouses under jackets.

•

Do not wear wide belts that fit tightly around the waist. Instead wear no belt or wear a matching narrow belt.

•

Choose softly tailored skirts.

•

Stay away from clinging fabrics and bright patterns.

•

Wear clothes that fit. If an outfit is not too tight and not too large, it will automatically make you appear thinner. Too tight an outfit makes you look heavier and very uncomfortable.

•

Downplay your figure-problem areas by not defining them. Since a snug-fitting sweater will call attention to a full or small chest, wear an easy-fitting top with a jacket that makes the problem less noticeable.

•

If you have bow legs, wear skirts that are a little longer and softer and fuller rather than skirts that are a straight line.

•

Choose vertical lines rather than horizontal lines.

•

Don't camouflage problem areas with a dull outfit but instead add attractive accessories at the neckline or add an attractive blouse.

•

Shape with lines and darts.

•

Use only subtle patterns and designs in clothes.

•

Use vest accents.

•

Avoid patterns or prints that are too bright, too small, or too large. Some of the prints that are made into clothes would look better in wallpaper than on someone's body.

•

Avoid mannish styles.

•

Avoid hairstyles that are too high or too short. A small hairstyle on a larger body does not always create an attractive proportion.

Choose loose clothes with tops that fall from the shoulder and give the illusion of softness and length.

The best lines to create a slimmer illusion are soft lines and flowing fabric.

•

Be aware that some vertical stripes can add width if they are too wide and are the same width across the body.

•

Make good use of tunic tops and jackets that come over the hip to cover the largest part of the hipline.

•

Wear solid colors or small designs and be careful of the larger prints. They can add width.

•

Wear a great hairstyle and keep a touch of color at your face so that the attention is focused on your face and away from your figure.

•

Do not wear two-color outfits.

•

Two-piece outfits in one color or in blended colors can add height and be slimming.

•

Be careful when wearing shiny colors as they will emphasize size.

•

Do not wear oversized collars, cuffs, and wide shoulder pads that will add width to a figure as well as horizontal lines.

For the full figure, well-made clothes are a must so spend a little more and get quality instead of quantity. Also, be aware of your posture. An erect and correct posture can help several figure problems and make you look your best. The full-figured woman's clothing needs to fit perfectly, especially through the shoulders.

Slacks

The correct pants outfit can camouflage large hips. It is a matter of knowing the best type of pant and how to use the lines to camouflage.

Sometimes two or more problems may contradict each other. If that happens, then dress for the problem that is most prominent.

——— ❧ ———

Wear a loose third layer over pants.

•

Thick waistlines can wear slacks if they are dark and solid in color, which is more slimming, and if they are combined with a V-neckline vest that will minimize the waistline.

•

A long-look illusion can also be achieved by wearing pants and jackets in matching colors.

•

Keep your pants pleat pressed sharply.

•

Choose loosely fitting and straight-legged-style slacks.

•

Soft pleating in the front of pants or a skirt can help hide the tummy bulge.

•

Do not wear jeans that fit too tight. Be sure that you look at yourself from all angles in a full-length mirror because some women's thighs are not even noticeable until they put on a pair of jeans.

Full-Figured Coats

———— ❧ ————

Do not try to hide under a heavy winter coat with bulky fabric because the wrong coat style often exaggerates the parts of the figure you do not want to emphasize.

•

If you have large hips then look for a loose body-slimming coat. If you choose a slightly padded shoulder line then the bigger and broader silhouette at the top will draw the eyes up and away from the hip area.

•

A stand-up collar also focuses attention upward and frames a pretty face.

•

Use vertical details such as set-in pockets and high armholes to help create a more slender look.

•

If you have a large bustline avoid garments with pockets in that area

•

It is best to avoid the boxy look of an untailored coat. Select a soft-draping good-quality wool.

•

The pleating on a coat should begin near the shoulder line so that it does not draw attention to the hips by making them a focal point.

•

If you have extra pounds then forget about the heavy down or quilted coats. They look good on the ski slopes but in general they make even the slimmest people look heavier. Horizontal quilting has a widening effect.

———————————— ❦ ————————————

If you have a heavy bustline, a wrap style coat can be good for you.

Be careful that your coat is not too short because this gives the upper body an oversized appearance and will accentuate problem hips and thighs.

•

When choosing a coat, avoid oversized collars, broad lapels, large cuffs, and wide shoulder pads that will add width to a figure as well as horizontal lines.

•

Do not choose coats with elbow patches and cuffed sleeves because they add extra thickness and make the arms look heavier.

•

If you have hip problems, you will want to avoid a coat that hugs the hipline, a wrapcoat, or anything that ties at the waist.

•

A V-neckline closure coat is best because it will elongate the neckline

•

A coat without a collar or a lapel is good because it eliminates one more layer of fabric where you do not need it.

●

Avoid shoulder pleating and puffed sleeves.

●

If you choose a belt, be sure it is narrow to eliminate a bulky, constricted look.

●

A slimming line in a coat fabric is a small vertical stripe or a small print such as a herringbone or tweed.

●

A basic and neutral color is best because it will go with all the clothes in your closet. If you have a large clothing budget then you can add some coats in different colors to extend the wardrobe.

●

Analyze your wardrobe for color. Black may be basic for some but perhaps your basics are beige or navy. A coat in your best basic color would work well throughout your wardrobe. Remember that darker colors will diminish the size of the figure and lighter and brighter colors will call attention to a figure and make it look larger. Dark colors do not mean only black, navy, or dark brown but could also include colors such as maroon or dark purple.

●

If you have figure problems, then draw attention to your face with scarves, earrings, and your best colors.

●

Don't forget to add some fashion touches to your coat such as a beautiful muffler or brightly colored scarves, and if your figure is tall add a shawl.

●

Too much fullness in a long sleeve should be avoided by people who have broad hips or who are too short.

●

If you travel or drive around a lot, then consider a coat that is easy to wear getting in and out of a car.

•

If you are short then a coat with a simple shape with a minimum amount of detail is best.

•

Do not choose a raglan sleeve that will add a top-heavy look.

•

If you have a short neck and are large on top look for neat open collars and choose a coat that closes high on the neck.

———————

When buying a coat, think about your profession. For instance, if you work in an office, a more businesslike look in a coat may be best. If you spend most of your time at home with children, perhaps a tweed or a sporty look would be best.

Thick Waist

——— 🐚 ———

If you have a thick waist, avoid belts.

•

If your hips can take this look, wear a low-slung double-wrap belt over the hipline and it will draw attention from the waist.

•

A thick waist should avoid big dramatic buckles and wide cinch belts.

•

Some good styles for a thick waist are unfitted A-line overblouses, the chemise look, and the loose jacket.

•

Tunics are a good look also.

•

Draw attention from the waistline with pearls or jewelry.

•

Thicker waistlines should wear belts of the same fabric and color or no belt at all.

Tummy Bulge

If you have a tummy bulge then use accessories to draw the eye upward.

•

If you must wear a belt then keep it simple, toned to your outfit, and never too tight.

*The tummy bulge
can be concealed with overblouses,
tunics, Empire waistlines, boxy jackets,
and vests.*

•

Avoid pants and skirts that are too form-fitting both in material and style.

•

Soft pleating over the abdomen is better than a flat look that does not conceal.

•

Do not wear hip-hugging pants.

Short Women

There are 37 million or more American women under five feet four inches. Many of them get very frustrated at the current state of fashion, which caters to the taller woman. Short women are constantly hearing rules of what to do and what not to do and sometimes it is so limiting and frustrating that they end up with the same clothing look day after day.

Short women are bombarded with rules about dressing in one color to look taller and slimmer but sometimes this becomes very boring. Obviously, a bold and highly contrasting color combination is going to make you look shorter but many times blending the colors and even using a low-contrast combination may take some boredom out of your wardrobe. An example of a strong two-color combination which would create a shortening line would be a white blouse and a black skirt. While dark colors are more slimming and elongate the figure, bright and light colors tend to enlarge and attract the eye. To look longer or taller wear a solid color from head to toe rather than bold patterns or prints. Or choose a subtle color with a small allover pattern.

—— 🐝 ——

Be sure that your posture is good by standing and sitting tall and straight for this forms the basis for an attractive appearance.

•

The experts say that the best look is to have about one-third proportion on top and two-thirds proportion on the bottom.

•

Create an illusion of height with vertical lines in your wardrobe.

•

Vertical lines can be added with seams, buttons, trim, or even with a V-neckline. Wear one color or keep it blended.

•

Small proportions are important in the patterns chosen but consider wearing some classic patterns such as tweeds in multicolors, small herringbone looks, and small polka dots. Some great looks can be found in paisleys and small stripes.

•

If you want to wear layers without looking bulky then choose some of the lighter-weight fabrics like silks and soft wool jersey. Soft, graceful fabric is a great way to look taller since heavy fabric and bold designs can overpower you.

•

Do not wear an exaggerated dolman sleeve or batwing sleeve. When this sleeve flares from the waistline it will shorten your look. However, if you must wear this sleeve, choose a scaled-down version of the batwing sleeve and have it start just below the bustline keeping a defined waist.

•

Adding details at the shoulders is another good way to create a longer line.

•

A short-waisted woman will look best in a narrow belt that is the same color as the garment she is wearing or is a subtle contrast. If you are long-waisted your belt can be wider but never so wide that it will make your legs look shorter.

•

Shawl collars will make you look taller by bringing the eye to your neckline.

•

The set-in sleeve and V-neckline are two lines that are the least shortening.

•

One rule for looking taller is to keep the fashion simple and uncluttered.

•

The softly gathered or dirndl skirt is a nice line for women who are short if the waistband is not too wide and the fabric is not too bulky. Choose a fabric that is soft and flows nicely such as challis or silk.

•

Pants that have a drawstring should be loose and never too full or overgathered. Wearing them tapered or medium straight in the leg is better than too full in the leg.

•

The blouson jacket should be more narrow with controlled fullness on top and should have a slim, not full or puffy, sleeve.

•

Wear slimmer shapes in skirts and coats rather than full or broad ones.

•

Avoid large collars or overly wide shoulders.

•

Puffed shoulders can add height.

———————————— 🙰 ————————————

It is best for the short woman not to use too many contrasting colors to accessorize.

Choose narrow rather than wide trousers and remember that slim does not necessarily mean tight or skinny. It simply means clothes that skim the body easily without clinging or a soft flow of fabric with no constriction.

•

The thinner the fabric, such as jersey or soft wool, the more gracefully it will fall.

•

A good thing to remember is that lengthening or shortening a skirt or top even by one-quarter inch can make all the difference in the proportions that are right for you.

•

For the long slim look, begin at the top by lengthening your neckline with standup collars, etc. Light attracts the eye and keeps the attention of the observer, so if you want to look taller or keep attention off of the hip and waist area wear something lighter toward the neck.

•

Be cautious of largely padded shoulders which will only add volume and width instead of height. A tiny bit of shoulder padding can give a lift to your height and make you look taller.

•

Complete your outfits with attractive accessories but wear them mainly at the neck level or higher. Earrings also keep attention focused high as do flattering hairstyles and makeup.

•

Drop shoulder styles work well when they are made of a soft, unlined fabric.

•

Do not wear a cuffed trouser, ankle strap shoes, ankle bracelets, contrasting border hems, horizontal stripes at hems, or midcalf-length pants or skirts.

•

To avoid bringing undue attention to your legs, stay away from color contrast between your stockings and skirt. If you keep your shoes, hose, and dress in one color or blends, you will look much taller.

•

If you are short and heavy do not wear heavily textured hosiery.

•

If you want to add length to your legs, the general rule is to always keep the darker tones on the bottom and the lighter tones on the top.

•

Open or V-vamp shoes and pumps are great for making your legs look longer as they show more of the upper foot and create an unbroken line.

•

A good dress for someone who wants to look slimmer and taller is the clean-line chemise. It has no belt, just a soft, straight, fluid flow from shoulder to hem. This works well for the woman with waist and hip problems because the line bypasses those areas.

•

The Empire waistline is another good choice to add height.

•

Add a slimming piece like a long knit vest, a jacket, or even a cardigan.

•

If you are a small person, do not wear a bold print that can overpower you.

———————

There are always many different changes in fashion as the seasons come and go but an important rule to remember when picking a new look is to dress to your own scale and proportion. Sometimes a new fashion can be very overwhelming to a short person but you can still wear it if you scale it down to your size.

Simply by shifting the center of interest in an outfit and placing the emphasis on other areas, you can fool the eye of the observer by balancing the design lines of your garment to the best outlines of your figure. For instance, you can give a strong impression of being taller by choosing a straight silhouette with a long look. Always look in a full-length mirror and your eye will let you know immediately if you are in balance with the fashion you are wearing.

Tall Women

Most of the time, the tall woman should just enjoy her height and enjoy looking good in the high fashion of the season. The key for a tall woman to look attractive is having good posture, which seems to be a problem for some women in this category. It does not matter how wonderful an outfit might be, if a tall women has a slumped and rounded shoulder posture, the fashion loses its look.

Tall is at least five feet six inches or taller. Because of your height you can wear many details such as ruffles, big buttons, pleats, gathers, and large cowl collars. At this height you can show off details without looking cluttered or overwhelmed. Some of the more noted taller women are Princess Diana, Cheryl Tiegs, Lynda Carter, and Brooke Shields If you are tall, you are in good company.

The taller woman has a greater number of options in the creation of a line. Height is an automatic asset for the taller woman and shows clothing to its best advantage

One problem that a tall woman discovers is that ready-to-wear sizes may not fit because sleeves are too short, pants and skirts are too short, or the waistline is in the wrong spot. If this is your problem, shop around for a certain brand name that will meet these problems and then stick with that brand.

——— 🐦 ———

The perfectly proportioned tall figure has a hipline that falls at one-half the total height and knees that fall at one-quarter the total height.

——————————— 🐦 ———————————

Do not buy items that have to be altered too much. They lose the general look they were designed to create.

If you are tall and perfectly proportioned, you can wear strong horizontal lines, cropped pants, broad shoulder styles, wide belts, and long jackets.

•

If you are long-legged you can wear a drop-waisted dress, an overblouse, a jacket which is hip length or longer, or a skirt hem up to the knee or mid-knee to break the long-legged look.

•

When you are tall you can have a lot of fun with color by wearing layers of contrasting separates.

•

A tall woman can make the most of bold prints, spectacular border prints, big scarf prints, and vivid Hawaiian screen prints.

•

Big plaids as well as wide stripes work well for the slim, tall woman with good proportions.

•

Even if you prefer not to draw attention to your waist, have fun with big interesting buckles.

•

The taller slender woman can wear a greater number of accessories than a woman of lesser stature. Use these accessories to focus attention on some of your best features.

•

Hats are a wonderful accessory and frame the face beautifully on the taller woman.

•

Lace jabots and large shawls and scarves are some effective looks.

•

Jewelry can be used in large amounts by the taller woman so use dramatic jewelry to create a super look that cannot be worn by all women. Consider layering your jewelry and using scarves.

•

Use the larger handbags for a great finishing touch to any outfit.

•

You can shorten the upper part of your figure by wearing short jackets or wide belts.

Thin Women

It is an interesting fact that most women, no matter how slim they are never feel thin enough. This can be a real obsession for some women because this society puts a strong emphasis on the model thin figure. However, there are a few people whose metabolism or genes are geared to being thin.

It has been said that you can never be too rich or too thin. But the truth is you can be too thin, at least for some styles of clothing. However, almost all clothes look better when they are draped on a slender figure.

—— ❧ ——

If you are bony in certain areas then stay away from straight skirts, skin-tight jeans, or skin-tight stretch pants.

•

Tops should have soft, full lines.

•

Halters, low necklines, bare midriffs, and short shorts will all emphasize thinness.

•

Wear full-cut clothing to fill out the curves of your body.

•

Use textured fabrics.

•

To add some roundness to areas, wear fabrics such as terry cloth, cable knits, and some soft wools.

•

Add shoulder pads to some loose-fitting jackets, blazers, pull-over sweaters, and cardigans.

•

Tuck your sweaters into your skirts and slacks to make your body look rounder and your hips appear flatter and smoother.

•

Choose blouses with smocking, large collars, and puffed sleeves to create the illusion of roundness.

•

Dress in the layered look with vests, blouses and sweaters, dusters, and jackets.

•

Wear wide contrasting belts and cummerbunds.

•

Jackets that stop at the waist with contrasting pants would be an interesting look for someone thin.

•

Experiment with accessories such as scarves tied in big floppy bows around your neck.

•

Avoid high hairdos and high hats if you are short and thin.

•

Pants of all types look great on the tall, slender figure. To add fullness at the hips, try pants that are pleated at the waistline.

•

If you are thin with no hips, wear skirts with graceful fullness and garments that soften the line of the hip like loose over-shirts, or an open shirt jacket and softly gathered slacks.

Skinny Legs

———— ಜಿ ————

Textured and knit hosiery are very good for the thin leg.

•

Herringbone and diamond patterns are good for daytime. Wear lacy designs for night.

•

Contrasting hosiery will make the leg look larger.

•

Hosiery in the classic taupe and suntan do not call attention to a leg whether it is too large or too small.

•

Darker nylons will make the leg look thinner.

Proportion and Line

Many women today go shopping without any idea of what their proportions are (where they are long and short), and consequently many clothes end up in their wardrobe without being worn because of what they do to their figures. Proportion is very simple. Essentially, it means that you make one section of your body look longer or shorter, narrower or wider, or larger or smaller. For example, wearing a high waistband either in slacks or a skirt will make your legs appear longer and the upper portion of your body will appear shorter.

Be aware that lines are very deceiving and if used correctly can take inches off or can add height. This can be accomplished with seams or prints in fabric. The eye follows the line so if the line is horizontal it will widen; if it is vertical it will slim and add height. Horizontal lines emphasize width especially when they are repetitive but they can create an impression of length depending on where they are placed. An example of this is a drop-waist dress. This lengthens the upper body.

Most of us do not have perfect proportions so we need to look for clothes and accessories that are harmonious with our body structure. Have you ever bought something because it looked great on a friend or a model in a magazine? Perhaps you found it to be very costly when you make purchases without considering your own proportions and body structure. Each person's body has a slightly different set of proportions. Even if you happen to be the same weight and height as someone else, chances are your proportions are not the same. Therefore, a design might be perfect for one woman and totally wrong for someone else.

—— 🐚 ——

Details such as border prints, ruffles, piping, buttons, and anything similar that carries the eye horizontally or vertically are considered a line.

•

When we do not feel good about the way we look, we draw attention to our figure flaws by our posture and our awkwardness. Learn all about your figure and learn to dress in a manner that makes you feel good so you can put your best foot forward.

•

One good way to train your eye regarding proportion and what it does, is to study the store windows, fashion magazines, and people on the street, and try to figure out why a particular outfit looks balanced or unbalanced.

•

Consider these items in determining what is best for you: color, details, width and length, textures, and the basic line of an outfit. With an awareness of what is best for you and the ability to put it into practice, you will find that you can shop easier and put details together that will create a well-balanced fashion look.

•

If you use a blouse or jacket with shoulder pads to make you look wider on top, it will make your hips look more narrow. Just remember that lines are very deceiving and by cleverly using line and color you can emphasize your most positive features and play down your negative ones.

•

Think about collars and lapels when you are purchasing a dress, suit, or coat. They should be scaled to your height and your size. Examine the lines of the collar to determine what they will do to your shoulder width.

•

Some other lines you should consider are seams, weaves of fabric, details, and necklines.

•

The length of a skirt or dress depends on how you feel when you see yourself standing and sitting in front of a full-length mirror. Usually the best length is one to one and one-half inches below the heaviest part of the leg.

•

A focal point that brings the eye upward to focus on your face could be earrings, makeup, or a ruffled neck blouse. A skirt with a slit or a high-heeled shoe will place the focal point at your leg.

•

Do not put all your focus on a good feature if it also exposes a poor feature. For example, do not wear dainty shoes on small feet if it will make you look out of proportion when you have extra weight.

•

Use focal points to draw attention away from figure flaws. Jewelry when used against a dark dress can draw attention away from your figure and jewelry used against a light background can call attention to your figure.

•

A yoke that has gathers will have a softening effect on broad shoulders and can also have a great balancing effect on narrow shoulders.

•

Soft gathers below a yoke can balance and camouflage a full bust if those gathers are not too bulky.

•

Soft gathers can also be used to make a small bust not as obvious.

•

To make the shoulder look broader use the wider and shallower neckline or the wider collar and lapel.

•

Yokes, jewelry, scarves, horizontal topstitching, and shoulder pads are all helpful to the narrow shoulder.

A longer jacket will make your legs appear shorter while a short jacket will add length to your legs.

To make the shoulder look more narrow, draw attention to the center with longer necklaces, buttons, scarves, more narrow and deeper necklines, inset sleeves, and narrow lapels.

•

The set-in sleeve is good on all body types and gives a balanced look to the body.

•

Only the well-proportioned individual should wear a sleeveless garment or halter neckline. A halter neckline will make a broad shoulder look much larger and a narrow shoulder look much smaller—just the opposite effect from what you want.

•

Always consider the texture of your material For instance, a cable knit sweater will add more width to the upper body than a lighter weight sweater.

•

Curved lines such as a soft draped look will do the same thing as straight lines and will hide many figure flaws. These line can emphasize the curves of your body and create a soft and more feminine appearance.

Necklines

With all the beautiful accessories out today that adorn the neckline, it is important for you to know how to make the best of your neckline beauty.

As we mentioned before, if you do not know if you have a long or short neck, draw an outline of your head, neck and shoulders on your mirror with some lipstick or a bar of soap. You will be able to see your proportions clearly. You can do this also to determine what face shape you have.

In choosing a proper neckline in a garment, consider the width of your shoulders and balance that with the width of your hips, length of your neck, and the shape of your face.

——— ❧ ———

If you have a dowager's hump at the base of your neck, choose collars that are set away from the neck in the back.

•

If you have a long neck, a dowager's hump, or poor posture, you will need help when wearing a neckline with no collar. Use scarves, jewelry, or an extra lay-on collar to achieve some balance and to camouflage.

•

Any line that you do not wish to emphasize in your face, do not repeat. An example would be if you have a square jaw, then do not wear a square collar.

•

If you have a thick short neck it will look more in proportion if you wear a collar set away from the neck instead of a collar like a crew or turtleneck that hugs close to the body.

•

Long thin necks will look better in higher collars and choker necklaces

•

A softly tied blouse is a good way to hide lines that are on the neck.

•

A scarf that is tucked into the neckline and some colorful beads that hang low will draw attention away from the neck.

•

A long neck is usually an asset and most of the top models have this feature. But if you have one that is exceptionally long and thin, try to create an illusion of fullness at your neckline with your hairstyle. Consider the hairstyle that is best for your face and if your neck is not one of your best features you can camouflage it with fashions.

•

A jewel neckline is an unfinished neckline that you can add accessories and designs to such as buttons, topstitching, and scarves. The jewel neckline is a very simple look. However, if you have a bony neck, a jewel neckline will not look the best on you without adding some softness.

•

A narrow collar that stands up can be worn by most figure types and also most people can wear a mock turtleneck unless their neck is extremely short or heavy.

•

A turtleneck is best on the medium to long neck.

•

More women are able to wear the softer type of fabric rather than the heavier look at the neckline.

•

Bows that are tied at the neckline create a softness around the face. Soft fabric will fall softly without too much bulk. Practice tying your bows so that they are not lopsided.

•

If you have a long neck you might try wrapping the ties around your neck for a more sophisticated look instead of tying them in a bow.

———

Even the correct lines and colors discussed here can give an unbalanced look if used incorrectly, so examine your figure, your good and bad points and start using this knowledge to dress correctly. Lines in clothing are very important because they carry the eye in a certain direction and will emphasize certain areas of your body.

20

Choosing a Swimsuit

Therefore honor God with your body.
—1 Corinthians 6:20

On a hot day, nothing beats a dip in a cool pool, but many women will not put on a swimsuit because they feel self-conscious of their figure. There are some things that can be done to look your best in a swimsuit. Lines are very deceiving so use them to achieve a certain look. Slim areas with vertical lines and widen areas with horizontal lines.

Don't be intimidated about going swimming when there are so many wonderful bathing suits in every style. Choose the one that is best for you.

General Tips

When looking for a suit, be sure that it is sewn correctly. For instance, the neckline should have no gaps and if the back is low, it should hug the body.

•

Swimsuit straps should leave the shoulder blades free to move for swimming but not so loose that they fall down.

•

Look for double or reinforced stitching at the straps, sides, back, and legs.

Heavy —Thick waist, too much hip, and tummy bulge

—— 🙿 ——

Choose a blouson top that softly drapes over the waistline and top of the hip.

•

Avoid ruffles, lace or any detail around the waist or hipline that would draw attention to that area.

•

Soft diagonal shirring over the waist and tummy area can help hide not only the waist but the tummy bulge.

•

Soft skirting can help hide tummy bulges.

•

White and brighter colors add inches. Choose a one-piece suit with descending colors such as navy and black.

•

If you are heavier than you wish, then do not choose a material that is too shiny or too bright.

•

Do not choose large flowers, horizontal lines, or bold patterns.

•

The V-neckline cut would be the most flattering to create a vertical line and more height and slimness.

•

Do not choose gathered skirts over the hipline because it will add extra bulk and inches.

Good Figure but Short Legs

—— 🙿 ——

A suit cut high at the leg adds length to the bottom half of your figure.

•

Do not choose suits that have a skirt that cuts across the top part of your legs.

•

Choose vertical striping to add leg length.

Too Thin

—— ❧ ——

Add some width with horizontal stripes. Two-tone striping is also good.

•

Choose a fabric that has more bulk than the nylon suit.

•

Choose a suit with prints and more design than most people can wear.

•

Bikini suits are not good if you are too bony.

•

Suits with skirts that add bulk and width are good for a thin figure.

•

Look for square necklines, soft boat necklines, and rounded necklines.

•

Choose the soft-flow diagonal lines.

•

Wear the brighter, more ascending colors and shiny fabrics.

PART 6

Special
Occasions

CHAPTER
21

Looking Good at Your Wedding

My soul rejoices in my God. For he
has clothed me with garments of salvation...
as a bride adorns herself with her jewels.
—Isaiah 61:10

Wedding Clothes Tips

Now that you have set the big date, it is time to start thinking about what you will wear when you walk down the aisle. It is important to look your very best on your wedding day so choose a dress that will emphasize your better figure features.

A wedding dress is a very important and expensive purchase so it is a good idea to plan what is best for you rather than to just do random shopping. There may be many beautiful gowns but if they do not bring out your most positive figure assets, then they will not look beautiful on you. Learn about your figure and what looks best and then you will feel very comfortable and self-assured on your wedding day.

———— 🦋 ————

If you are short and slender:

•

Choose a simple design line that will draw the eye upward and give you an illusion of height.

•

Choose a long tapered sleeve or a single ruffle on the sleeve.

•

Avoid too much clutter as it will shorten you.

•

Choose a dress that is close to the body and avoid one with too much fullness.

•

Choose a lightweight fabric.

If you are short and not slender:

Choose a higher neckline.

•

Choose a long tapered sleeve.

•

Choose a fabric that is not bulky.

•

Look for delicate to medium trim.

•

Do not choose a shiny fabric.

•

Keep a soft flow in the fabric.

•

Choose the Empire waistline for a good line.

If you are tall and slender:

You can choose textured fabrics.

•

Use trim and appliques that go around the body such as ruffles.

•

Choose full sleeves.

•

Look for softness and fullness. You can wear those styles that will show off a model figure. An exception might be the Empire line which would add more height.

•

You can wear most fashions and add high fashion touches.

If you are tall and not so slender:

Stay away from short puffy sleeves.

•

Do not use heavy trim.

•

Use the vertical lines rather than the horizontal lines.

•

Do not choose a shiny fabric.

•

Avoid too much bulk.

Some of the traditional wedding fabrics are satins, taffeta, crepe, and brocade, along with lace and sheer overlays. A romantic fabric that is less traditional is the pique, organza, eyelet, or the semisheer handkerchief linen. When choosing fabrics remember that crisp fabrics generally create a sculptured shape and the soft fabrics create a fluid line.

When you choose a wedding gown, keep in mind that people will be seeing you both from the front and back so consider what is flattering from both angles. If you have a derriere problem you will not want to add to it by wearing a bustle of some sort. Also consider the neckline and bodice both in the front and back to emphasize your best features. See figure section in chapter 19.

Whenever handling a wedding gown, be sure that the area as well as your hands are clean. Also, be sure that your nail polish is dry. A bottle of seltzer may be used for emergency stains and a can of hairspray for any lipstick that may get on the gown. Be sure that you test it on an inconspicuous area first to make sure that it will not show.

CHAPTER

22

*Packing
for Trips*

*Go in peace.
Your journey has the Lord's approval.*
—Judges 18:6

This is the age when men and women are traveling more and more, and sometimes deciding what to pack can really become a hassle. If you are about to embark on a trip or vacation, it is a good idea to give some forethought to your needs and be prepared.

Preparation

Choose a hairstyle that is easy for you to manage on the trip.

•

About a week before your trip, check the weather at your destination. You can also check the long-range weather forecast.

•

Get organized on paper by making a list of the days that you will be gone, what you plan to wear each day, and where you are going to wear it (swimming, dinner parties, meetings).

•

Make a list of everything that you pack and keep it with you so that if you lose anything you will have an easier time making a claim. Also, making a packing list a week in advance will allow for dry cleaning, etc. This will take a lot of stress out of last-minute preparations.

•

On the last day before your trip, eliminate everything that you absolutely do not need. Many times the things we chose at first can now be easily eliminated.

•

When packing, get together a "be ready for anything" kit. Pack a few things for emergencies and unexpected situations such as purse-sized tissue, wash-up towelettes, rubber bands, shower cap, aspirin, and suntan lotions. Purchase the smallest size possible of these items and be sure to put them into unbreakable containers.

•

Pack your makeup in a special bag. As you use each item the morning of your trip, pack it and then nothing will be left behind. Buy some pretty plastic-lined cotton bags for your cosmetics and one for your medications and vitamins.

•

Do not take anything on a trip that you have never worn. A trip is not the place to break something in.

•

As soon as you return home, restock your little bags with such essentials as a small shampoo, toothpaste, extra toothbrush, laundry soap, and other little extras that you may have depleted. This will help cut down on the last-minute rush before your next trip.

•

Start packing a few days before you are going to leave. Do not leave it to the last minute.

•

Keep your bags open in your bedroom so whenever you think of something you need, you can stop and pack it.

•

If you wear glasses, take along an extra pair and also a copy of your prescription.

•

Bring a sewing kit and safety pins.

•

Always take along prescriptions for medicines in case you need them. If you are traveling abroad, the customs officials may question drugs that you have packed or it may be difficult to get a refill in a strange city. It is also a good idea to carry your medications and essential cosmetics in your handbag or a small tote and keep it with you so that you will have them should your luggage end up in Hong Kong and you in Los Angeles.

———————————— ❧ ————————————

In order to handle your own baggage easier, pack in two smaller suitcases that you can carry yourself rather than one large one.

If you travel a lot, get yourself a portable luggage dolly or buy the suitcases with wheels and pull handle. Test them to see that they pull easily.

•

Use some personalized identification markings on your baggage that can be easily seen so that they do not get picked up by someone else who has similar luggage. Some brightly colored tape or yarn around the handles is easily recognized.

•

Do not use your name and address as an ID mark. Put your name and business address on the concealed flap or keep it inside the bag. There are people called spotters at airports who love to find names and addresses of people going out of town. It gives them time to go and clean out the traveler's apartment or home.

•

Use some canvas safety belts around your luggage to prevent them from coming open.

•

The most efficient way to travel, if you can, is with carry-on pieces only. Take a canvas duffel that will fit under the seat, a shoulder-strap bag, and a garment bag with handles so you can fold it and carry it easily.

Clothes

———— 🙝 ————

•

Check to see how many combinations you can make so that you do not have to take as many clothes. Try to stay within your basics and neutrals and add one major color. Knowing your color key comes in handy because everything that you put together will coordinate in color and fashion. If you do this, you will need fewer accessories as well as less makeup and nail polish. An example would be to use one color scheme such as black and white, then add brighter accessories to perk them up. If one piece you have packed does not go with at least three other items, leave it behind. Keep it simple.

•

Use your layering techniques to go from daytime into the evening without a complete change.

•

Remember that what you wear on the plane should be included in your coordinated pieces.

•

Take some items that are easy for you to wash and drip dry.

•

If you will bring a lot of accessories such as belts, scarves, and jewelry, you can create a multitude of looks. Many times you can just change the jewelry on an outfit to change it from day to evening. Add a pair of evening shoes and you are set to go.

•

Take a black or navy basic dress to wear simple in the daytime and with some elegant jewelry and heels at night.

•

Do not take expensive pieces with you that could be lost or stolen.

•

Take shoes that are easy to walk in and one pair of dressier shoes. If you decide to take your boots, then wear them to save space.

•

Never break new shoes in on a trip. Take your most comfortable shoes.

•

Take garments that do not wrinkle, are lightweight, and will hang out when you get to your destination. A lightweight gabardine is a good fabric because it can be worn in all seasons. Many times if you will hang these kinds of fabrics in the bathroom during your shower, the steam will take out any wrinkles.

•

Cottons and cotton blends pack well and are relatively fuss-free.

•

It is a good idea to pack a lightweight nylon raincoat.

•

Avoid looking too bare when visiting big cities.

•

A robe is very bulky so do not pack it unless long, cozy evenings are planned.

Packing Tips

—— 🐝 ——

When you pack, zip, button, and belt a garment before you pack it and it will lay flatter and become less wrinkled.

•

Match the leg seams of your trousers and then fold them in half.

•

Try to weave your clothes together so that they are snug in your suitcase and then they will not shift as much and there will be less wrinkling.

•

Place all heavy items like your hair dryer, cosmetic kit, jewelry roll or shoes on the bottom of the suitcase opposite the handle so that when you lift the suitcase the heavy items do not drag the clothes with them as they fall to the bottom.

Slip your shoes into some old cotton socks to keep them from soiling your other clothes or your suitcase.

Save space by rolling some of your items like lingerie, T-shirts, sweaters, and knits and fit them snugly along the suitcase front.

•

Stuff small items like belts and socks into shoes.

•

If you will pack one complete outfit together, you can unpack it without disturbing the other pieces.

•

Stash a collapsible bag or foldable water-proof nylon bag into your suitcase so that you will have something to hold your souvenirs.

•

Wastepaper basket liners are great for packing sweaters, blouses, and shoes. Use dry cleaner bags to slide over larger pieces of clothing before folding. Plastic holds air and helps to cut down on creases.

•

Use stockings and small items such as scarves to stuff shoulders of jackets and blouses.

•

Fold crushable items like silk over cushions of sweaters.

•

Pack skirts and dresses inside out so that the creases will be inverted and will not show as much.

•

Put pants, skirts, blouses, and dresses on a thin hanger and each in a plastic cleaning bag. Then fold them into thirds and when you get to your destination you can just pull out the hangers, shake the clothes out, and then hang up.

•

Pack last what you will use first.

•

Safety pins come in handy for hanging skirts and slacks.

Packing a Garment Bag

—— ❧ ——

Learn to layer four or five garments on a single sturdy hanger.

•

Fold one or two pairs of trousers over the garment bar, put skirts flat over pants, and then add a dress folded lengthwise down the middle

•

On another hanger, layer your blouses four to a hanger. Button the top button of each and stuff tissue paper in the sleeves.

•

Jackets or coats go onto a hanger over everything else

•

Sweaters, like pants, are put over the hanger bars. This will allow you to pack the maximum amount of clothing in a bag.

―――――――

Do not pack everything you love to wear, just in case, because chances are that most of it will have to be lugged back home unworn. Planning is the key word.

CHAPTER

23

Don't Be Afraid to Entertain

*Do not forget to entertain strangers,
for by so doing some people have entertained
angels without knowing it.*
—Hebrews 13:2

One of the great privileges of life is to have people into your home and to enjoy great fellowship with them. It is important to put away the concerns you may have when you entertain, especially the concern that says everything must be perfect in your home before people can come in. Most people just wish to have your companionship and it can give you a lot of pleasure to be able to serve them and make them feel like they are the most special people while in your home. People just want your friendship and your company so put away some pride and entertain with a servant's heart. People need to be shown that they are special to us and that we are glad to be with them.

The number one purpose when we have guests into our home is to make them feel at ease. The smile that we give them and the warmth of a hug both give off this message.

General Tips

━━ 🐦 ━━

•

If you are having dinner, make it pleasing with a nice table setting, a tablecloth, and an attractive centerpiece.

•

Centerpieces might include flowers, fruit, some nice candles, or a combination of these. If you do not have room for this type of setting, then improvise but don't stop inviting people just because you don't think you can make it fancy. Some of the nicest entertainment is done buffet style.

●

Set a mood for your dinner party because when you create an environment that makes you happy, it will create a happy atmosphere for your guests. It is nice to have something aesthetically pleasant to set a mood, like scented candles or the smell of potpourri.

●

Do not cook something exotic or special that you have never prepared before. Fix something you have made many times.

●

Use shortcuts as much as possible such as a dish that you can prepare days or even weeks ahead of time. It is always easier to have a menu that can be prepared before the big day.

●

Be organized and get things done ahead of time so that the joy of the occasion is not marred by stress and anxiety or pressure. Some people get so involved in the preparation of food they forget that the purpose of the party is to be with their friends. The food should help the guests enjoy themselves but it should not be the most important ingredient of the party.

●

Always serve your guests first and watch for when they need refills so they do not have to sit without water or something that would make the meal more enjoyable.

●

If you served something that was highly successful, then write it down and why it worked so well so that you can fix it for other guests. It might be good to note who you have served it to so that you can avoid repeating a meal with the same guests.

●

Get your spouse involved in the planning or plan a party with a friend and share responsibilities.

●

Be flexible in your decorating ideas. You do not need a lace tablecloth and crystal glasses to set a wonderful table.

●

Candles are especially effective for a nighttime party. It is fun to use a few or to put them in groups. Use interesting candle holders such as cored apples.

•

Do not wait to have people in until your house is perfect because if you do you will be missing some memorable times.

•

If you do not feel up to having a large dinner party, then start small with a few friends for dessert.

———————

When you have a party of any kind, forget yourself and concentrate on others. Then you will feel more relaxed and will enjoy yourself.

A Few Simple Etiquette Rules

Etiquette is often misunderstood because everyone thinks it involves rigid rules or impossible guidelines, but it really means simply being kind to each other.

If you are kind and gracious, you will automatically be on your way to practicing the rules of etiquette.

Get acquainted with some of the simple rules of etiquette because you will automatically feel more at ease when you know what to say or do. Here are a few that cover the basics.

——— ❧ ———

Do not put your napkin on your lap until grace has been said or the hostess starts the dinner. In a restaurant, do not take the napkin until the order has been given.

•

The man's napkin goes over one knee.

•

Do not shake a napkin out full but keep it folded in half. The exception would be a small luncheon napkin which you can open completely.

•

Use utensils from the outside in.

•

Do not cut your meat into many small pieces but cut one piece at a time and eat. Cutting into many pieces is like cutting meat for a small child.

•

Scoop soup from front to back.

---

*When eating a roll,
tear instead of cutting. Break off
a bite-size piece, butter and eat.*

Use your napkin to blot lipstick so that there are no lipstick marks on the glass. Do not drink until your mouth is empty so that particles of food do not get into the water.

•

Do not stab the food but scoop your utensil under the food and eat. The exception is lettuce which can be stabbed with the fork and then eaten.

•

Bread can be used as a pusher but do not use your finger.

•

Never put a used utensil back on the table. Keep it on the plate and when you are finished eating, the utensils should be placed at twelve o'clock or four o'clock on the plate to indicate the plate can be taken away.

•

If you drop a utensil on the floor, do not pick it up and put it back on the table. Wait for the waitress or hostess to pick it up.

•

Do not pick your teeth at the table. If you must get something out of your teeth, go to the bathroom to remove it.

•

If you must leave the table before the meal is finished to answer the phone, leave your napkin on the chair.

•

Do not fold a used napkin up nicely but place it to the side of your plate when the meal is finished.

•

To remember how to remove plates and how to serve, think R for "remove from the right," and therefore you would serve from the left.

•

Start serving the food to the right and after it has been served once, it can be passed either way.

•

You have heard all your life that it is impolite to put your elbows on the table. You will find, however, that it gives a warmer feeling if you have one arm resting on the table and you lean a little forward to visit with others. Do not put both elbows on top of the table and rest your head in your hands.

———

It would be good to purchase an etiquette book to get a more in-depth look at proper etiquette. If you do not know the rule for something, just remember that common sense should come into play and if you use that with some thoughtfulness you will rarely ever be guilty of bad manners. Manners are ways of behaving with polite standards but etiquette is a set of rules set up for proper social behavior and developed with thoughtfulness for the other person in mind.

PART 7

Growing Older with Grace

24

Caring for Your Beauty As You Grow Older

*She is a woman of strength and dignity,
and has no fear of old age.*
—Proverbs 31:25 TLB

While we are all aware of growing older, we shouldn't worry about it because these years can be some of the best years of our lives. Some of us grow older gracefully, some of us do not. When we were 20 years old we thought that we would be young all of our lives, and then all of a sudden 20 or 30 more years have gone by. If the body and mind are taken care of, you can remain strong physically and mentally; however, it does take work. There may be a few more gray hairs and a few more wrinkles, but learning to accept these changes can give you a more positive look on maturing. Fortunately, there is a new attitude about older people now and about what they can and cannot do—but mostly about what they can do.

How do you maintain a positive, joyful attitude about aging? Some people really enjoy the latter years and some simply bear them. It is a choice. God gave us this wonderful power of choice. We can choose to be just as miserable or as happy as we want to be by the way we look at the process of aging. Abraham Lincoln said, "We can be as happy as we choose to be." Certainly circumstances enter in but how we deal with the circumstances makes the difference. A truly happy and glowing person, older or younger, is someone who is satisfied in all aspects of life.

General Tips

Beauty begins on the inside both physically and mentally. I think our attitudes have more to do with what we do with our age than any other factor. Some older people think that everyone owes them something just because they are old. Some think that they can talk and act any way they want, but if you want to be pleasant to be around and to be someone whom people admire, then check your attitude toward yourself and your age.

——— ✿ ———

Spend some time playing and just enjoying life. It is wonderful to be a great success but it is also good to give yourself permission to enjoy some leisure activities.

•

Develop some very rewarding relationships that add to your satisfaction and fullness of living.

•

Try to cut down on things that cause stress in your life because stress causes aging and is a drain on your body and mind. You might try taking some deep breaths, getting regular amounts of exercise, and listening to your favorite music to help relieve stress.

•

Trusting that there is a God who loves you and cares for you gives you a serenity that nothing else can duplicate. Regular periods of prayer and watching your faith increase bring a real glow to your countenance.

•

Develop a hobby that is pleasing to you and that is relaxing. Some hobbies cause more stress than they are worth.

•

As we get older posture is extremely important. Be aware of how you walk, sit, and stand and make an effort to keep your body in alignment. Having a springy gait in your walk will take years off of your age.

•

Be sure that your vitamin, mineral, and calcium intake is not being depleted, which can cause a hardship in getting around as you get older. Get a good checkup with your doctor.

•

Keep your nails and hands looking younger by sticking to medium earthy or rose shades. Dark or bright polish draws attention to spots.

•

A noted voice teacher says that if you talk with energy, it will make you ageless.

It is important as you get older to stay committed, involved, and right in the mainstream of life.

Even the fashions that you wear have a lot more to do with how you see yourself and the shape you are in than they do with age.

•

Aging is an inch-by-inch process so neglect of yourself may not be noticeable at the moment, but over a period of time the wear and tear will build up and become increasingly noticeable.

•

One recent statistic said that 85 percent of people over the age of 65 have no real physical problems. The older generation is keeping themselves fit, staying healthier and looking younger than previous generations. Start your physical fitness and nutrition program today.

•

Use your mind by studying and reading and you will stay sharp a lot longer.

Hair

Two mistakes that many older women make are that they keep their longer hair and their deep red lipsticks. Unfortunately, these only add to their age. It is important to stay with the times and make changes that will bring out your best features.

—— ❧ ——

Get your hair styled in a shorter cut for a more youthful look. Most hairdressers agree that too long a hairstyle or one that pulls the face downward is actually quite aging. As we get older we need more of an uplift in our hairstyles. After 40 it is best to keep the hair a little shorter, simple, and not too trendy.

•

Keep your hair in some of the more moderate color tones. Lighter colors are less aging so instead of coloring your hair too dark, try having the lightest strands brightened a shade or two.

•

Use good moisturizing conditioners on your hair to fight the dryness and lack of luster that comes with age.

•

Do not be afraid to color your hair if you do not like gray hair. Some women look good in gray hair but on others it can be very aging.

Fashion

Pretty colors are one of the easiest ways to put together an attractive wardrobe because a closet full of dull, safe solids can add years to your fashion look. Add a healthy amount of lively colors and prints and it will give you a much younger look.

—— ❧ ——

If you want to dress with more authority without an older look, wear finer quality and more sophisticated subtle lines.

•

Wear subtle colors unless you look really smashing in a bright color like electric blue.

•

The sophisticated and geometric prints are better than the large floral prints.

•

Add some softer fabrics in blouses for a younger look. The men's tweeds or strict pinstripes seem to give the oldest image. A younger fashion in a suit is the short jacket bloused or fitted to the waist, or a peplum jacket. A soft flare over the hip with the peplum gives a younger look because they are soft compared to the larger out-of-proportion jackets. The figure, however, needs to be slim to wear this.

Makeup and Skin Care Tips

Be aware of your facial expressions because bad habits such as a frown, a squint, or a scowl can leave its mark on your skin. The collagen understructure weakens from the continual expression and a wrinkle becomes etched into the skin. Catch yourself when you begin to tense up your face and consciously relax those muscles. It is never too late to turn some bad habits into good so start today.

Skin Care

—— ❧ ——

Smiling deepens the lines from outside the nostrils of the nose to the corners of the mouth, whereas squinting will give crows' feet a good start. Pursing your lips causes vertical lines along the top lip.

•

Long-term ultraviolet light damage can cause wrinkling, leathery skin, and broken capillaries. Since cellular repair decreases with age, the older you get the less efficient your skin is at repairing the damage. Ninety-five percent of the wrinkles that show up on your skin are caused by the sun.

•

The fairer your skin, the thinner your skin and the earlier you will show signs of aging. Begin protecting your skin early in life and be aware that a tan is not good for your skin at all. You will need the most protection on the thinnest and driest areas of your face such as your eyes, neck, and cheeks.

•

One big factor in adding more wrinkles to the skin is cigarette smoking. Anytime you have something that affects your body in a negative way, it will also affect your skin negatively.

•

Be sure that you establish a sound skin-care program such as a good moisturizer for the face and body.

•

The two most important things to help keep your skin from aging are cleaning the skin gently and protecting it adequately.

•

If you want to avoid unwanted facial wrinkles then sleep on your back so that you do not push wrinkles into your face.

———————— ❧ ————————

Heredity also plays a part in aging,
so your parents' faces can provide
a good visual look at how you will age.

If you clench your teeth or tense up your face when under stress, you will show aging lines.

•

There is no reason why at age 50 or over your skin should not be soft and supple and your hair shining and healthy. Nevertheless, menopause does take its toll on the condition of your skin and hair as some of your hormones decrease. At this time a good facial scrub is important to ensure that your skin texture remains smooth and glowing. The skin is drier and more delicate so use only the mildest of scrubs.

•

The throat and neck area tend to age rapidly so always start moisturizing from the collarbone up. Some neck exercises would be good also, such as opening your mouth and tightly pulling the bottom jaw up in an exaggerated chewing motion.

•

Spray some water on your face and then apply your moisturizer with a gentle patting motion. Finish getting dressed while this soaks into your face. You do not have to buy the most expensive moisturizer to get good results.

Makeup for the Mature

The 20-year-old can wear makeup or skip it altogether, but by the time we reach our thirties more makeup is needed for a more defined look. In the forties our makeup needs to be a bit softer and by our fifties we usually know our best qualities and what to accent and what to soften.

Makeup is a form of fashion and changes with the times so take the current ideas and adapt them to what is best for you.

One of the most aging mistakes made is when a woman uses the incorrect color in a makeup base and then carries that color into her clothes selection. The reflections from the wrong color will cause sallowness in the skin and then her wrinkles will become more obvious.

As we get older, some of the beauty tips that we used a few years ago may not be the best for us now. We all change with age and so should our makeup. Every beauty expert has her own opinion about what is best, but you need to consider who you are and what is best for you. Here are a few tips.

———— ❧ ————

Jet-black eyeliners are more aging than a softer line, so use the softer charcoal pencil and smudge it in.

•

Shaggy brows accent sagging lids and deep lines.

•

Check your liner and brows to be sure they are the same thickness on both eyes.

•

A thicker eyebrow gives a more youthful look than the thin-plucked line or penciled-in brow. Fill in with a soft stroke of eye shadow for a natural look.

•

Brow powder is best and is less harsh than brow pencil

•

Frosted lip, eye, or cheek colors accentuate wrinkles so it is best to switch to a lighter foundation and stick with more smoky shadow colors.

•

The foundation should be just enough to even out your skin's appearance and should closely match your complexion. Choose a foundation that is close to your natural color, which may be a little lighter than it was when you were younger. Older skin loses color as well as moisture so a foundation is important to even out the skin tone.

•

Always blend foundation well around the edges so you do not have a line on your neck.

•

Loose powder will help to minimize hard lines. As you age, do not use iridescent powder because it will exaggerate lines and wrinkles.

•

Older eyes do not look their best in heavy makeup. Color on a craggy lid is not attractive, especially colors such as blue, green or turquoise which are some of the most unbecoming colors. Stay with the soft muted shades and ones that will not accentuate the eye. If you have a craggy eyelid, use creamy powder and apply it to the lid using your finger.

•

When we get older, it is best to stick to the subtle neutral shades.

•

Reappraise your makeup colors about every five years to see if they are still giving you the best look for your age

•

As the skin ages, the face becomes drier and more lined. This will make the foundation sink into the skin and accentuate the lines around the eyes and mouth. If this is a problem, choose subtle colors for your eyes and lips to counteract the grayness.

•

Apply a thin layer of moisturizing foundation with a damp sponge and then cover with a soft translucent powder.

•

Keep your foundation to the barest minimum around the eyes where wrinkles are easily emphasized.

•

Although the creamy lipsticks moisturize the lips, women who are older should wear the no-smear lipsticks instead because the creamy ones will tend to get into the wrinkles around the mouth and accentuate them. Lip liners will help to eliminate this problem.

•

If you go on a crash diet, which many women do, you make the problem worse by losing muscle tone with the result being a sagging appearance

---

Cosmetics can subtract years from the face but they need to be applied more carefully in the older years. Layers of foundation and face powder can be very aging because they can settle into the creases of the skin bringing out every line, so use a lighter hand when applying makeup. Remember, simplicity is better. This doesn't mean that a woman is better off with no makeup at all. Nearly every woman needs to wear an under-eye concealer and foundation which will smooth out the imperfections in the skin.

There are some women of 40 that look 30 and some who are 30 that look 40, which says a lot about the importance of taking care of ourselves. It helps to have good genes but even if we do and do not take care of our skin, it will eventually catch up with us and heredity does little good.

Exercise

Exercise is very good for your skin because it increases circulation and promotes the delivery of oxygen and nutrients to the skin as well as removing wastes. It is hard to get into the habit of exercising and to have the self-discipline to do it often enough to accomplish its purpose, so choose an exercise that you enjoy and do it You will be glad you did and it will pay dividends

Take responsibility for your own health and make it a priority if you want to preserve your looks for the advancing years. As you get older you tend to lose muscle and gain fat and the result is a middle-age spread. The key point is to start a good form of exercise as a regular regimen to build muscle.

———— ❧ ————

Do not start an exercise program without some information and instruction on what is best for you.

•

When you begin an exercise program, begin slowly and build up gradually. If you do not exercise in mid-life, then the joints will stiffen and your body will function less efficiently.

———————— ❧ ————————

*The experts say that
if you exercise at least
three or four times a week,
you can expect good results.*

Replacing fat with muscle through a proper diet and exercise program allows you to carry more weight.

•

If you are losing weight, then do it slowly enough so that the skin does not get saggy and wrinkled. If you do it slowly, the skin can adjust to the fat volume loss.

•

Eat a balanced diet. A lot of women eat the same amounts and types of food in mid-life as they did as teenagers and then they do not understand why they no longer weigh the same. The problem is as we get older our metabolism slows down so that the body burns fewer calories in its resting state. This means you need to eat about a hundred fewer calories a day for each decade after 40. Once again, proper diet nourishes the whole body including the skin.

•

Walking is one of the best exercises for older people. It can be done inside a mall or school and it causes the least damage to your knees, backs, and feet.

Sleep

Relaxing is essential to beauty and getting enough sleep and rest will help your wrinkles and give you a refreshed look. This may not be possible for some people, but a 15-minute rest in the morning and in the afternoon can be a great refresher. This is a rest period without visiting or interruptions.

——— 🍂 ———

If you have a hard time going to sleep, try rising earlier in the morning and continue doing this until you are sleepy at your bedtime hour.

•

Go to sleep when you are tired, not when it's time to go to bed. Everyone is a special individual and sleep needs vary from person to person.

•

If you feel wide awake, capitalize on having some extra time to do some things you want to do.

•

Fresh air and gentle exercise are two good sleep inducers particularly if they are done just before bedtime.

•

Do not eat too much food just before bedtime.

•

Some of the experts say that cheese, milk, and yogurt are all good night foods.

•

Milk is especially good as a nighttime food because it contains high levels of amino acids which seem to play a significant part in producing sleep.

•

High carbohydrates before bedtime are not good.

•

Do not take stimulants before bedtime such as alcohol, chocolate, sugar, salt, coffee, tea, or cola drinks. These may act as a metabolism stimulant for up to seven hours.

•

Check your surroundings to be sure that you are comfortable in bed. You may need a new mattress if yours is too hard or too soft.

•

Check your background noise and see if that may be disturbing you without your realizing it.

•

Sleep in a bedroom away from street noises.

•

Make sure that your windows are fitted tightly. It is easier to fall asleep in a crowded room with all the windows shut because the amount of oxygen available is gradually being displaced by carbon dioxide.

•

Take time to unwind before going to bed by listening to soft music, reading, or looking at something pleasant.

•

Learn to prioritize because you may have said yes when you should have said no to an activity that causes you undue stress and sleeplessness.

•

If you have trouble getting to sleep, try this relaxing tip. Run a warm but not too hot bath. Put on some soft music and add your favorite scented cologne or bubble bath to the tub. Put moisturizer all over your body before getting into the water. Then drink a glass of warm milk while you soak for about 10 minutes. When you get out you will be ready for a good night's sleep.

PART 8

Men Are
Important Too

25

Making the Most of Your Dollar with Clothing

The steps of a good man are directed by the Lord.
—Psalm 37:23 ᴛʟʙ

Success is ambition, talent, experience, good judgment, dedication, skill, and some luck, but the key that often opens the way for a man to show what he can do and gives him the confidence to do it is his appearance.

You know what your qualifications and abilities are but the client or employer has to guess and most of the time what they have to judge by is the appearance and grooming of the man.

Tips for Men in Purchasing a Suit, Jacket, or Trouser

The suit is the uniform of success in the business world and when building a wardrobe with a look of success you should choose the look that identifies you with the leaders in your field. Lapels should be considered when purchasing a suit because too wide or too narrow a lapel can be very dating to a suit. If you deal with a reputable retailer, you can be assured that the suit he sells will be in keeping with the current trends. Be careful that you don't get caught with an out-of-date look. Invest in quality because economy is achieved by building your wardrobe with some durability and versatility in mind.

Shorter Men

——— 🙖 ———

A man who is short will look best in vertical lines in both the pattern and the cut of the suit.

•

Buy jackets that are a little shorter because a long jacket makes the legs appears shorter.

•

A shorter man will look best in pants that are a slim cut and are not cuffed.

•

Shoes should blend and belts should be the same color as the pants.

Heavier Men

——— 🙖 ———

A heavier man should not wear bright colors or bold patterns.

•

Thin-striped suits and vertical designs are good.

•

Do not wear clothes that are too tight.

•

Coats should be slightly longer than average.

•

Vertical lines in ties are important.

•

Wear dark colors and fabrics with a flatter finish.

Slimmer and Taller Men

——— 🙖 ———

A slimmer and taller body can wear plaids and checks

•

Wear a two-color combination in jacket and pants.

•

Choose coats with broad shoulders.

•

These men look good in jackets that are loose-fitting at the waist.

•

Double-breasted suits are wonderful for the tall slim man.

General Business Suit Tips

A high price tag does not always reflect quality in men's clothes, but usually you get what you pay for.

—— 🐝 ——

Solid-color suits are the best purchase and then you can add some tweed jackets, slacks, and nice soft striped shirts and ties that are purchased with color coordination in mind.

•

For a first purchase, a solid-color vested business suit in a good wool blend is best. Even though vests may not be worn predominantly that particular season they soon will be in fashion again and you will always have it available. A vest should fit smooth and close to the body without the slightest sign of pulling or creasing.

•

The more contrast that you have the greater the air of authority you will give to your client, such as a navy suit and white shirt. If you do not want to be as intimidating and have a friendlier look, choose a medium-shade suit such as a medium blue, which is best in sales.

•

A blazer in tweed or a good wool blend is appropriate for some business occasions and can be worn on all informal occasions.

•

It is not the best look to mix and match suits and sport coats or wear a suit coat with sport slacks

•

The navy blazer and gray trouser are always a good fashion and business look and would be a good addition to any wardrobe. The navy blazer is an important mainstay in a man's wardrobe.

Trousers

———— ✿ ————

Purchase a garment that needs few alterations, because too many changes can camouflage rather than correct the problem of an ill-fitting garment. Do not be afraid to have some alterations, however, to make the garment look tailor-made.

•

Clip a small piece of fabric from the inseam of the trouser and jacket and put it on a 3x5 card. Then take the card when shopping to match your ties, jackets, shirts, and slacks.

•

The waistline should fit comfortably and there should be enough fabric to not pull at the derriere, thighs, hips, and across the lower abdomen.

•

The break of the trouser or how much fabric rests on the shoe should be no more than one-half inch.

•

Select some conservative colors that will coordinate with your other major wardrobe pieces. Gray, navy, and a touch of burgundy are good examples.

Jackets

Develop a keen eye for details in the line of the garment and check the fabric closely. A jacket is going to be a major purchase and should coordinate throughout your wardrobe. If you have a lot of blue in your wardrobe, then it would not be wise to get a jacket with too much brown. In other words, be sure that your tweed, plaid, or any other multicolored jacket has the most predominant color in your wardrobe in it.

Learn to look closely at the interior of the suit jacket or sport coat and you will see the kind of construction that makes for a comfortable and nicely hanging jacket. Critiquing the interior of a suit jacket is as important as examining the outer appearance.

———— ❧ ————

Mitered corners (one that forms a v) are the sign of a well-made jacket.

•

The sleeves should have enough fabric to be lengthened if needed and the armhole should be cleanly finished.

•

One thing to observe when critiquing the interior of a jacket is the center seam down the back. It should have one-half inch of extra fabric on both sides of the seam. This seam is a folded seam and is necessary for any alterations that may be needed.

———————————— ❧ ————————————

Three or four pockets inside the jacket are a sign of quality.

—————————————————————

The inside of the collar should be lined, but the lining should not extend past the edge of the collar.

•

There should not be a gap when the jacket is buttoned. Check to see that the jacket hangs with the natural body line.

•

The best jacket sleeve length should show a little of the shirt sleeve, about one-quarter to one-half inch. This is a general rule. The correct sleeve length for a jacket measures five inches from the end of the sleeve to the tip of the thumb.

•

Jackets that are made of a good-quality wool will usually be a good buy.

•

When trying on a new jacket, raise your arms above your head, then bring them slowly down to the sides. This will settle the jacket onto the shoulders and enable you to judge a good fit. If the fabric bunches in any area, this may indicate that the collar is not laying properly. Notice the back of the jacket. Vertical wrinkles or creases indicate the jacket is too large. If it has horizontal creases, it is an indication that it is too tight.

•

Diagonal lines along the back of a jacket indicate that the opposite shoulder is too low which is a common problem and can be corrected with padding.

Coats

Take into consideration what fashion image you wish to portray before you purchase a coat or sports jacket. Take into consideration the climate, where you live and work, how much business traveling you do, where you go, and what type of clients you deal with the most. If you give some forethought to this, you can then purchase perhaps only one or two sport coats to cover all of your needs not only for keeping warm but also for looking good.

——— ❧ ———

Select a coat that is in a solid color or a conservative pattern. When you do this, you are less likely to be in a position where you would have to wear a bold-patterned coat with a distinctively patterned suit or trousers.

•

Raincoats or trench coats with zip-in liners are the best buy for every man's wardrobe. Either offers year-round protection from inclement weather and is the ideal coat for travel.

•

Raincoats or trench coats are not a substitute for the tailored coats for the man dressed for success. Most importantly, choose the right coat for you and the image you want to project.

•

The best business color for the successful look in a raincoat is a neutral beige or taupe.

Shoes

—— ᥒᜈ ——

Shoes are an important purchase and should always coordinate in color to the pant you are wearing.

•

Shoe experts say that the weight of the body is divided between each foot with 50 percent on the heel, 30 percent on the big toe area or ball of the foot, and 20 percent on the little toe area.

•

A wide toe-box with sufficient height is important for proper weight balance. A narrow toe area squeezes the toes together diminishing balance.

•

Men's shoes should be classic, flattering, and well-polished. White shoes are not good with suits unless you want people to look at your feet first instead of you.

•

Good fashion means coordinating the color and texture of your shoes and belts. For example, do not wear a black belt with brown shoes or vice versa.

•

Shoes, belts, and hats should be hung on a rack to keep them looking as nice as possible.

•

When you are out of shoe polish and your shoes are a mess, try rubbing in a small amount of hand cream and buff to a bright shine.

•

Try linseed oil on the soles of squeaky shoes to eliminate the noise.

Socks

—— ᥒᜈ ——

Argyles, crew socks, and whites are for sport and leisure wear only.

•

Small neat patterns in socks are correct for business as long as they do not clash with the color or pattern in your suit.

•

If a camel or tan shoe is worn with the coordinating suit then wear camel or tan socks.

It is best to wear black socks with all dark shoes.

When you sit down for a business meeting, the look of success is not three inches of hairy calf showing, so be sure your socks are showing instead. A nice over-the-calf or mid-calf sock is the proper length for a neat business look.

Shirts

A small pattern or a narrow stripe in your shirt will coordinate with many ties. If the stripe or pattern is bold, it would be best to wear a solid tie.

•

The best business shirt is white, solid color, striped, or pale-hued. Do not wear deep solid colors for a business look, such as deep burgundy or green.

Ties

The tie is one of the most important things that a man wears because it can make a man look successful or unsuccessful. Ties mean respect, show credibility, show individuality, and are a fashion statement. They provide an important finishing touch for any business or dress wardrobe, so think what image you are wanting to portray when putting on your tie.

Remember a tie should harmonize in color with the outfit and the pattern in the tie should not conflict with the pattern of the suit or sport coat. If you combine a plaid suit or sport coat with a strongly patterned tie, the look seldom works.

•

Squiggly ties or loud ties do not give off an air of success.

•

The darker the tie the more authority the man gives off, but black ties should be worn only to funerals. The exception to this is evening wear; for example, a black bow tie with a tuxedo.

•

Solid colors in ties in conservative tones are good as well as ties with the repeat stripes, polka dots, and small diamonds. The ties with the regimental stripes are ideal for the businessman and for selling. If a man can afford only one tie, then buy the repeat-striped tie.

•

The width of ties can vary from year to year but the determining factor in which tie is right for you is that the width should be in direct proportion to the width of your suit lapels. The wide tie with a narrow lapel destroys the harmony of an outfit and the same thing applies to a narrow tie with a wide lapel.

•

The bow tie is not a businessman's tie.

•

Never wear your tie tied in a small tight knot. It should be tied just firmly enough to keep it in position.

•

When purchasing a tie, the silk or silk blends are best because they tie better and do not make a large knot.

•

When hanging your ties, always hang them without knots from a tie rack to prevent crushing them or getting them wrinkled.

•

Do not wear white ties for business.

•

Some food stains will come out of ties if you rub a little talcum powder on the spot and leave it overnight. Then gently brush it off in the morning.

Accessories for Men

Accessories are important for men as well as women. One basic rule for men's jewelry is the less the better. Too much jewelry or the wrong kind of jewelry can bring negative responses.

——— ✌ ———

Tie clips should be relatively expensive or at least have that expensive look. A cheap tie clip can ruin the best tie.

•

Tie tacks are popular but be careful because they can make holes in your expensive ties.

————————————— ✌ —————————————

*Wear lapel pins
only if they have significance
such as an honor.*

Some men can wear tasteful ID bracelets, but most of the time they do not work well, especially for a business look.

•

Cuff links should be simple and the expensive gold or silver are the best. Do not wear gaudy cuff links.

•

Handkerchief pocket squares should match or harmonize with your tie or shirt and they can add a smart touch of color.

•

When choosing a belt, buy fine leather and be aware of the belt buckle. The big heavy ornate buckles are not as acceptable for business as the small clean traditional buckles with squared lines. The larger ornate buckles are mostly worn with western wear.

•

Wallets should be the finest leather and fit flat in the back pocket without a lot of bulge. The finer the leather, the better it will work for your overall presence.

•

The best color for wallets is a dark rich brown or deep burgundy.

•

The larger, longer, pocket secretary wallet that can be carried in the suit pocket is very useful for the man who wears a lot of suits.

•

An attaché case should be made of fine leather and is usually quite expensive but worth the extra money. It is a positive symbol of success regardless of what the man is carrying in it and it always lends presence to a man. The best color to purchase is the dark rich tone of brown leather or deep maroon or burgundy. Black and gray do not look as rich. Attaché cases should be simple and functional without a lot of decoration or hardware on them.

Casual Wear

The leisure time in a man's life is very important. The clothes he wears for leisure are a big part of keeping that image of success. Relaxing does not mean that a man's appearance has to be less than the standard that has made him successful in the first place. A lot of business is done on the golf course, tennis court, or at a dinner party.

When selecting leisure clothes, choose them on the basis of comfort, function, and to suit your personality. A man can wear the brightest, most colorful apparel when wearing this type of clothing. Patterns and fabrics run the gamut from bold to conservative. What is right to wear is determined by the occasion and location as well as the season of the year.

Here are some tips on what to wear to feel the most comfortable in various situations

———— ð⊛ ————

An afternoon party in the fall would lend itself to a nice pair of corduroy slacks, a sport shirt, and maybe a sweater.

•

An evening at the country club would call for a more dressy look such as flannel slacks and a sporty jacket with a shirt and tie.

•

For an art show or casual outing, wear jeans and a sport shirt or even a light jacket or sweater and some comfortable walking shoes. The idea is called relaxing in style.

———————— ð⊛ ————————

Choosing a golf or sport outfit is where you can find some of the most beautiful colors for men.

Jogging and running have become so popular that they have developed fashions of their very own. Joggers no longer wear the old gray sweatshirt but instead you now see many well-styled sweats worn with matching jackets.

•

Racquetball players should dress as colorfully as tennis players.

————————

Sweaters are a great look and add beautiful colors as well as patterns in a great many varieties. Look for one that is not only warm but fashionable as well.

Time Tested Fashions for Men

There are several fashions for men that are time tested—that is they are classic and have been around for many years without change. These fashions would be good purchases because they are not fads and they will look up-to-date year after year.

One example of a time-tested outfit is the oxford shirt, a pair of khaki trousers, a sweater, a navy blue blazer, and the popular penny loafer. These would be good purchases and a man might get many years of use out of them without ever being fashion dated.

The smart man will buy a few high-quality, well-made classic garments rather than buying several inexpensive and faddish items. Good clothes not only last longer but are also more versatile.

The way we dress and our outward appearance does make a difference not only in how people look at us but in how we feel about ourselves. Right or not, first impressions affect how we think of people.

If you are skeptical about how clothes can affect your image think about how the television industry not only uses clothing but hairstyle and color to produce a certain kind of character for their movie or advertisement. It has been shown that long hair in women is very sensuous, blonds have more fun, and that gray hair on a woman no matter how lovely she may be makes her look older; however, gray hair on men makes them look distinguished. Glasses add an air of authority and make a man look like a bookworm or at least like he is very intelligent.

Grooming and Skin Care for Men

If the Lord delights in a man's ways, he makes his steps firm.
—Psalm 37:23

A well-planned, good grooming routine is vital to the man who cares about his appearance. Whether it is short or long, a good cut and clean hair are essential. An unkempt haircut will make you look ragged all over. A man's appearance should be as simple and uncomplicated as possible.

Also, men need healthy complexions as well as the woman. If a man will take good care of his skin he can have a glowing complexion.

———— 🐛 ————

Since after-shave has alcohol in it, the scent will not linger as long as you may desire so use some body talc in the same scent to extend the aroma (Do not use the talc on your face because it will clog your pores).

•

Some skin experts suggest to their clients that they have a professional facial at least four times a year.

•

Follow a daily cleansing and moisturizing program at home.

•

To help the wrinkles that develop under and around the eyes, use a good eye cream.

•

Daily bathing or a shower is essential.

•

Always use deodorant. There are many on the market and you can purchase products that match the fragrance in your after-shave. Be careful not to wear too many scents at the same time. The deodorant should complement the other fragrances used.

•

Fragrances, hair and skin preparations, and bronzes help to give a man that confident feeling. There is nothing wrong with a man wanting to look as attractive or as young as he can.

A Few Hints for Shaving

Shaving is one of the main causes for differences between men and women's skin, making the men's skin tougher and more sensitive. The appearance of both men's and women's skin relies heavily on the blood supply and on the support of collagen and elastin; so if these things are kept in good condition, it will slow the aging process. Some other factors that contribute to the condition of the skin are diet, insufficient sleep, smoking, alcohol, drugs, seasonal changes, exposure to the sun, pollution, indoor heating, air-conditioning, and stress.

If a man will shave properly, it will help his face rather than harm it because it will help remove dead surface cells. The difference between an electric shaver and a razor is that the shaver clips the hairs off while a razor slices. Both can harm the face if not used properly on a carefully prepared face.

——— ❧ ———

Do not use a dull blade.

•

Use cream and gel preparations that work into the face and soften the facial hairs. The softer the hairs, the less irritation will result on the skin.

•

When using an electric shaver, the drier your skin is the better because this will cause less irritation and fewer ingrown hairs.

•

Do not shave an area over and over again.

•

Try to shave only once a day. If you must shave a second time, then use only an electric shaver.

— ૨ા —

If you will alternate between an electric shaver and a razor, it will help to reduce skin irritation.

If your skin gets particularly irritated, cease shaving for a while and grow a beard to let the skin rest.

•

Men can use a good moisturizing cream instead of shaving lotion if they need more lubrication and want a less drying effect.

Beards and Mustaches

Statistics show that the more hair a man has on his face, the less credibility he has. However, if a man is going to grow a beard or mustache, then it is important to keep it well groomed.

— ૨ા —

A new beard should be kept clean at all times. While soap and water is probably enough at the initial stages, later the beard should be washed with shampoo.

•

Cleanliness is imperative so that you do not harbor bacteria at the root of your beard.

•

If flaking occurs do not use dandruff shampoo. It is probably caused by insufficient rinsing after shampooing the beard or by not drying the beard correctly.

•

Do not use blow dryers to dry your beard because the heat is too intense for the tender facial skin.

•

Comb or brush a beard in the direction you want it to lie. This is almost always a downward motion.

•

Do not rub after-shave lotion or cologne into a beard or mustache. These products are usually alcohol-based and will cause the whiskers to dry out, robbing them of their natural oils.

•

Trimming beards and mustaches is easier when they are dry since you can see more clearly what you are clipping away.

•

To trim a full beard brush up and comb out and remove the tangles in the beard with your fingers. A rough comb or brush can break the hair and irritate the face.

•

If you want a shaped beard, be sure the line between the shaved and unshaved areas is straight, sharp, and clean.

•

If you are tired of a beard or mustache and want to remove it, first remove most of the hair with scissors before shaving because the razor pull can be too much for the skin and leave severe abrasions on your face.

Baldness

Men dread baldness as much as women dread a wrinkle. Thyroid and anemia are a couple of the causes for baldness and should be checked by a doctor. However, most baldness is found in the same family from generation to generation. The gene for the hereditary tendency to baldness is said to come from the maternal side.

———— 🐦 ————

Doctors say that there is no actual proof that changes in diet, or taking mineral and vitamin supplements, or using shampoos directly applied to the scalp can alter the course of hair loss. There is some controversy over this because some companies make other claims. One product promotes the theory that calcium builds up on the scalp keeping the hair follicle from growing and this product helps to cleanse and eliminate this problem. The theory is that if the pore of the hair itself is cleansed thoroughly and not plugged, then the hair will grow. Many men claim that they actually do find their hair growing healthy again when using some remedies, but doctors say the explanation may be that some of the stress is gone over the hair loss.

•

If it is a real problem in your life, there are some really wonderful toupees available that are almost impossible to detect.

•

Sometimes men wear large muttonchop sideburns to compensate for the loss of hair on top of their heads. Instead this style tends to throw off the entire balance of the face and can even emphasize what is missing.

•

Some men will grow their hair to almost shoulder length to draw attention away from their baldness; however this doesn't seem to work either. What looks the most natural is what is best.

•

If your hair is getting thin on the top, you can let it grow a little longer than normal, but to take long hair and try to comb it over the baldness only emphasizes the problem.

————————

The best way to beat baldness is to accept it and accept yourself and emphasize all your other assets. Maybe baldness is an asset to you. It didn't hurt Yul Brenner or Sean Connery.

Some Final Thoughts

Find a special place where you can take time for yourself, a special place where you can observe the wondrous creation, look at the sky, watch the clouds, and even inhale the beauty of a flower. How many times have you heard people say they have had to come close to losing their lives before they took the time to appreciate their surroundings and their families? Don't wait for some trial to come into your life before you stop and smell the roses. Take time to dream your special dreams.

When you take time to refresh yourself and seek God's plan and will for your life, you will find that you can give of yourself to your family and to the world with a whole new attitude and your true inner beauty can shine through.

• • •

Writing this book for you has been so much fun for me personally. When I was teaching and doing my radio show, there was a lot of response to the short, easy tips and thus this book was born. The purpose was to make looking and feeling good simple by giving you practical tips that are easy to put into practice without having to wade through a lot of research. If you will take the knowledge you have gained and use this book as a reference point, it will make your life easier and less stressful. Just turn to the chapter which will meet your need at that moment—from shopping to packing for a trip. Don't let this book collect dust but use it to help your life be a little less complicated and a lot more fun. The end result is that you will be more beautiful, both on the inside and the outside, to yourself and to the world.

Other Good
Harvest House Reading

MORE HOURS IN MY DAY
by *Emilie Barnes*

There can be more hours in your day when you use the collection of calendars, charts, and guides in this useful book on home time management.

SURVIVAL FOR BUSY WOMEN
Establishing Efficient Home Management
by *Emilie Barnes*

A hands-on manual for establishing a more efficient home-management program. Over 25 charts and forms can be personalized to help you organize your home.

THE 15-MINUTE ORGANIZER
by *Emilie Barnes*

The 15-Minute Organizer is a dream book for the hurried and harried. Its 80 chapters are short and direct so you get right to the answers you need that will let you get ahead and stay ahead when the demands of life threaten to pull you behind.

QUIET TIMES FOR COUPLES
by *H. Norman Wright*

Noted counselor and author Norm Wright provides the help you need to nurture your oneness in Christ. In a few moments together each day you will discover a deeper, richer intimacy with each other and with God, sharing your fondest dreams and deepest thoughts—creating memories of quiet times together.

QUIET MOMENTS FOR WOMEN
by *June Masters Bacher*

Though written for women, this devotional will benefit the entire family Mrs Bacher's down-to-earth, often humorous experiences have a daily message of God's love for you!

THE SPIRIT OF LOVELINESS
by *Emilie Barnes*

Join Emilie Barnes as she shares insights into the inner qualities of spiritual beauty and explores the places of the heart where true femininity is born. With hundreds of "lovely" ideas to help you personalize your home, Emilie shows that beauty *can* be achieved with even the lightest touch of creativity. Your spirit of loveliness will shine through as you make your home a place of prayer, peace, and pleasure for your family.

MOMMY APPLESEED
by *Sally Leman Chall*

In this delightfully written book, Sally Leman Chall shares her secrets from over 20 years of classroom experience as she helps parents make the most of the teachable moments in their child's life. Packed with hundreds of simple, creative activities that parents and children can do together, *Mommy Appleseed* is an invaluable resource for parents of preschool and early elementary school children.